cooking with
Cheese

cooking with Cheese

over 80 deliciously inspiring
recipes from soups and salads
to pasta and pies

RYLAND PETERS & SMALL
LONDON • NEW YORK

Designer Paul Stradling
Editors Alice Sambrook, Kate Eddison
Production Controller Mai-Ling Collyer
Art Director Leslie Harrington
Picture Manager Christina Borsi
Editorial Director Julia Charles
Publisher Cindy Richards

Indexer Hilary Bird

First published in 2016 by
Ryland Peters & Small
20–21 Jockey's Fields
London WC1R 4BW
and
341 E 116th St
New York NY 10029

www.rylandpeters.com

Text © 2016 Belinda Williams, Chloe Coker, Fiona
Beckett, Hannah Miles, Jenny Linford, Laura
Washburn, Liz Franklin, Maxine Clark, Miisa Mink,
Nicola Graimes, Ross Dobson, Shelagh Ryan, Tonia
George, Tori Haschka, Ursula Ferrigno and Valerie
Aikman-Smith
Design and photographs ©
Ryland Peters & Small 2016

ISBN: 978-1-84975-718-8

10 9 8 7 6 5 4 3 2 1

A CIP record for this book is available from the
British Library.

US Library of Congress CIP data has been
applied for.

Printed and bound in China

Notes

• Ovens should be preheated to the specified
temperatures. We recommend using an oven
thermometer. If using a fan-assisted oven, adjust
temperatures according to the manufacturer's
instructions.

• Both British (metric) and American (imperial
plus US cups) are included in these recipes; however, it
is important to work with one set of measurements and
not alternate between the two within a recipe.

• All eggs are medium (UK) or large (US), unless
specified as large, in which case US extra large should
be used. Uncooked or partially cooked eggs should not
be served to the very old, frail, young children, pregnant
women or those with compromised immune systems.

• When a recipe calls for the grated zest of citrus fruit,
buy unwaxed fruit and wash well before using. If you
can only find treated fruit, scrub well in warm soapy
water before using.

Contents

Introduction

Who can resist the primal call of oozing, golden, bubbly melted cheese? It is the magical food that can pep up the blandest of sandwiches, cure a hangover, ease a broken heart and even get a party started. In this collection of over 80 amazingly cheesetastic recipes there is something delicious for all ages and all occasions.

In a world where vegetarian options and #meatfreemondays are ever-rising in popularity, there is room for cheese to hold its own at the dinner table like never before. Though of course it is best friends with bacon too! One of the most versatile foods around, cheese is equally good served for breakfast, lunch, dinner and dessert.

A carefully selected cheese can transform a humdrum dish into gourmet grub and set the tone for the rest of a meal. Go French with Roquefort, Spanish with Manchego, Italian with Taleggio or Indian with Paneer. France, (the most cheese-consuming nation in the world) offers over 400 varieties of cheese alone, and there are thousands more worldwide in a wealth of colours and textures. Some cheeses can be made overnight, others are aged for months or years in a special environment to develop their flavour. With so much wonderful choice, it can sometimes be hard to veer from a safe favourite. Let this book inspire you to cook with a wider range of cheeses. Friends and family will love the crowd-pleasing gooey pizzas, risottos, pastries and luxurious cheesecakes, just right for a special occasion or wintry night. But it doesn't have to be indulgence all the way – discover how to enjoy cheese without piling on the pounds. Light and delicate cheeses like feta, mozzarella and ricotta are perfect for summer months in soups, salads and frittatas. Moreover, cheese is packed with red blood cell loving vitamin B12, as well as essential calcium vital to human growth and development. In fact the high protein content makes it an ideal post-gym snack. Yes really.

In this essential guide for cheese-lovers, all the best ways to enjoy cheese are laid bare. For now all that is left to wonder is, why did the cheese not want to get sliced? Answer: it had greater plans.

Small Bites and Appetizers

A punchy cheese is the perfect focal point for a small but tasty morsel. The Tapenade and Parmesan Cheese Straws are great for party nibbles and kids will love to snack on the Breadcrumbed Halloumi Goujons. To get an elegant dinner party started, try the Ricotta and Spinach Dumplings with Cherry Tomato sauce.

Goat's cheese and anchovy palmiers

These adorable little pastries are a take on the sweet pastries you often find in Spain, which are made in the same manner except with sugar. The cheese and anchovies give them a delicious salty bite, which makes them ridiculously addictive.

**a 500-g/17½-oz. pack
   puff pastry
100 g/¾ cup crumbled
   soft goat's cheese
50-g/2-oz can anchovies,
   drained and chopped
2 tablespoons freshly
   chopped thyme**

2 baking sheets, greased

MAKES 32

Preheat the oven to 200°C (400°F) Gas 6.

Cut the pastry in half. Take one half and put it on a lightly floured surface. Roll out into a rectangle approximately 20 x 30 cm/7¾ x 11¾ in. Spread with half the goat's cheese and scatter with half the anchovies and thyme. Repeat this process with the other piece of pastry. Roll the shorter sides very tightly into the centre and squash together tightly. Cut into slices about 2 cm/¾ in. thick and place on the prepared baking sheets. Flatten each slice well with the palm of your hand.

Bake in the preheated oven for 20–25 minutes until golden. Leave to cool on the baking sheets.

Tapenade and Parmesan cheese straws

If you like, you can spread these with Marmite/yeast extract, pesto or sundried tomato paste instead of the tapenade, and you can vary the cheese too. Or simply brush with butter and scatter with sesame or poppy seeds. They need eating up within a day or two after which they lose their crunch.

1 egg, beaten
2 tablespoons whole milk
a 375-g/13¼-oz. pack
   puff pastry
75 g/generous 1 cup
   Parmesan, finely grated
3 tablespoons black olive
   tapenade

2 baking sheets, greased

MAKES 15

Preheat the oven to 200°C (400°F) Gas 6.

Mix the egg with the milk. Cut the pastry in half. Take one half and put it on a lightly floured surface. Roll out into a 30-cm/11¾-in. square. Repeat with the other half. Brush one sheet with egg wash. Scatter with two-thirds of the Parmesan. Spread the other sheet with tapenade and place on top of the first sheet, spread-side down. Press gently and glaze again with the remaining egg wash. Cut into 1-cm/½-in. strips, twist several times and transfer to the prepared baking sheets. Scatter with the rest of the cheese and bake in the preheated oven for 15–18 minutes until golden.

Breadcrumbed halloumi goujons

Served warm and oozing with melted halloumi cheese, these breadcrumbed bites are hard to resist! To give them a little heat, add a pinch of hot smoked paprika to the breadcrumbs and serve with a cooling garlic mayonnaise.

50 g/⅓ cup plus 1 tablespoon plain/all-purpose flour, seasoned with salt and pepper

1 egg, lightly beaten

150 g/2 cups dried white breadcrumbs

a pinch of smoked hot paprika (optional)

250 g/9 oz. halloumi, cut into 8 slices

500 ml/about 2 cups vegetable oil, for frying

sea salt flakes and freshly ground black pepper

lemon wedges, to serve

garlic mayonnaise, to serve (optional)

a deep-fat fryer (optional)

MAKES 8

For the breadcrumb coating, put the flour, egg and breadcrumbs (mixed with paprika, if using), in 3 separate bowls. Take the slices of halloumi and coat them in flour, tapping off any excess. Next coat them in the egg and finally in the breadcrumbs. For an extra crunchy coating repeat the process.

If you have a deep-fat fryer, set the temperature to 160°C (325°F); if not, pour the vegetable oil into a deep stainless steel pan and fill no more than half-full with oil. To test the temperature of the oil, place a small piece of bread in the pan – it should take 10–15 seconds to turn golden brown.

Put the breadcrumbed halloumi into the hot oil and fry until golden brown (this will take 3–4 minutes). Dry off the halloumi on paper towels and sprinkle with sea salt. Serve warm with lemon wedges for squeezing and garlic mayonnaise for dipping, if liked.

Cream cheese and olive parcels

These delicious Mediterranean–flavoured, cream cheese–filled nibbles are the perfect appetizers to serve with drinks.

1 teaspoon olive oil

3 spring onions/scallions, finely chopped

200 g/1 cup cream cheese

40 g/⅓ cup pitted/stoned green olives, chopped

1 tablespoon finely chopped fresh dill

freshly ground black pepper

6 rectangular filo/phyllo sheets

50 g/3½ tablespoons unsalted butter, melted

sesame seeds, to garnish

a baking sheet, greased

MAKES 12

Preheat the oven to 200°C (400°F) Gas 6.

Heat the olive oil in a small frying pan/skillet and fry the spring onions/scallions until softened. Set aside until cool.

In a mixing bowl, mix the cream cheese, fried spring onions/scallions, olives and dill. Season with a generous grinding of black pepper.

Slice the filo/phyllo sheets in half lengthways, forming 12 rectangular strips.

Brush one of the strips with melted butter (keeping the remaining sheets covered with clingfilm/plastic wrap to prevent them drying out). Place a generous teaspoon of the cream cheese mixture on the buttered filo/phyllo strip 2 cm/1 in. from the bottom. Take the bottom left corner of the strip and fold it up and over the filling, to form a triangular shape, then across again to the other side. Continue until you have formed a tightly closed triangular parcel. Brush on a little extra melted butter to seal the last flap into place and then place on the prepared baking sheet. Brush the parcel generously with melted butter and sprinkle over a few sesame seeds.

Repeat the process with the remaining filo/phyllo strips, making 12 parcels in total.

Bake them in the preheated oven for 15–20 minutes until golden-brown. Serve warm or at room temperature.

Grilled halloumi with blistered jalapeño relish

1 lb./450 g halloumi
3 tablespoons olive oil
grated zest and juice of
    2 limes
Blistered Jalapeño Relish
    (see below)
cracked black pepper, for
    sprinkling
extra limes, for squeezing

Relish (makes 2 cups/
    16 oz./475 ml)
3 tablespoons olive oil,
    plus extra for oiling
4 jalapeño chillies/chiles
1 red and 1 white onion,
    thinly sliced
3 garlic cloves, finely
    chopped
1 tablespoon lime pickle
2 tablespoons tequila
3 tablespoons clear honey
¼ cup/60 ml white wine
    vinegar
sea salt flakes

*still-warm sterilized glass
    jars with airtight lids*

SERVES 6

Halloumi is a Cypriot cheese with a rich, salty flavour, and is perfect for grilling/broiling and pan frying. It has a mild taste so it works very well alongside strong flavours or sweet fruits, such as watermelon and figs.

Begin by preparing the halloumi. Slice the cheese into 5-mm/¼-in. pieces. Place a cast-iron pan over medium–high heat and pour in the olive oil. Swirl the pan to coat. Working in batches, add the halloumi and sauté on each side for 2 minutes. Add a little lime zest and juice to the pan for each batch. The halloumi will cook quickly, so don't let it brown too much. Transfer the cheese to a warm serving platter until needed.

To make the relish, place a lightly oiled large cast-iron pan over high heat until smoking. Add the jalapeños, lower the heat slightly, and cook until the skins are charred and blistered. Remove from the pan and set aside to cool.

Add the oil, sliced onions and garlic to the pan and cook over medium heat for 5 minutes, stirring occasionally. Season with salt to taste. Add the lime pickle.

Roughly chop the cooled jalapeños and add to the pan along with the tequila, honey and vinegar. Cook for a further 10 minutes, until the onions are golden brown and soft.

To serve, place a teaspoon of relish on top of each piece of cheese. Sprinkle with cracked black pepper and finish with an extra squeeze of lime. Serve immediately.

Tomato and ricotta roulade

This light and elegant concoction of ricotta cheese, tomatoes, eggs and fresh herbs makes a wonderfully summery dish. Serve it for a light meal, accompanied by a crisp green side salad.

40 g/2½ tablespoons butter

1 bay leaf

40 g/⅓ cup plain/all-purpose flour

300 ml/1¼ cups whole milk

3 tablespoons tomato purée/paste

3 eggs, separated

200 g/6½ oz. cherry tomatoes

300 g/10 oz. ricotta

4 tablespoons each of fresh finely chopped flat-leaf parsley, basil leaves and chives

1 teaspoon finely grated lemon zest

2 tablespoons grated Parmesan

salt and freshly ground black pepper

a 23 x 32-cm/9 x 13-in. swiss/jelly roll baking pan, greased and lined with baking parchment
a baking sheet, greased

SERVES 4

Preheat the oven to 200°C (400°F) Gas 6.

Melt the butter together with the bay leaf in a heavy-based saucepan set over medium heat. Add the flour and cook, stirring, for 1 minute, to form a paste. Gradually stir in the milk and cook, stirring continuously, until thickened.

Transfer to a large mixing bowl, discard the bay leaf and season with salt and pepper. Stir in the tomato purée/paste, to form a tomato roux. Beat in the egg yolks, one by one.

Whisk the egg whites until stiff peaks form. Stir a spoonful of the whisked egg white into the tomato roux mixture to loosen it. Gently fold in the remaining whisked egg whites. Carefully spread the mixture evenly into the prepared baking pan.

Bake in the preheated oven for 12–15 minutes until risen and set. Remove from the oven, cover with a clean kitchen cloth and set aside to cool.

Cut the tomatoes in half, scoop out the pulp and discard. Finely dice the tomato shells, leaving the skin on for texture.

Prepare the filling by mixing together the chopped tomatoes, ricotta, herbs and lemon zest, seasoning with pepper.

Uncover the cooled roulade and spread evenly with the tomato mixture. Roll up the roulade from the short side, forming a long roll. Transfer to the prepared baking sheet. Sprinkle the roulade with the grated Parmesan and bake in the preheated oven for 20 minutes.

Serve in slices warm from the oven.

Baked goat's cheese with honey-spiced beetroot/beet

The goat's cheese in this recipe is baked until soft and unctuous, and when served on top of the beetroot/beet salad it makes a perfect light meal or appetizer with slices of country-style bread.

8 uncooked red and
    golden baby
    beetroot/beets, washed
    and trimmed
2 tablespoons olive oil
1 tablespoon clear honey
1 teaspoon harissa spice
    mix
100 g/3¾ oz. rocket/
    arugula leaves
60 g/⅓ cup pea shoots
2 red chicory/endive
    heads, sliced
4 tablespoons freshly
    snipped chives
4 x 100 g/3¾ oz. goat's
    cheeses, halved
    horizontally

Dressing
5 tablespoons extra virgin
    olive oil
1 tablespoon balsamic
    vinegar
sea salt flakes and freshly
    ground black pepper

SERVES 4

Preheat the oven to 200°C (400°F) Gas 6.

Brush the beetroot/beets with 1 tablespoon of the oil and roast in the preheated oven for 30 minutes until almost tender. Mix together the honey and harissa with the remaining oil in a bowl, then season. Transfer the beetroot/beets to the bowl and turn until coated in the honey spice mix. Return the beetroot/beets to the roasting pan and roast for another 10 minutes or until tender.

Meanwhile, mix together all the ingredients for the dressing and season. Arrange the rocket/arugula, pea shoots, chicory/endive and chives on 4 plates.

Just before the beetroot/beets are ready, place the goat's cheese halves in a second roasting pan, skin-side down. Bake for 5 minutes until soft and starting to run.

Slice the beetroot/beets into quarters and arrange on top of the salad portions, drizzle the dressing over and top each portion with 2 halves of goat's cheese.

Baked ricotta with aubergine/eggplant and currant relish

This dish works really well because cheese and fruit is such a classic pairing. The indulgency of the creamy ricotta and flavour of the red wine and currants mean that it would be perfect for the festive season. For a bigger meal, serve as a tasty alternative side dish with a roast chicken and salad.

1 kg/5 cups ricotta
1 garlic clove
½ teaspoon sea salt
2 eggs, separated
1 teaspoon grated lemon zest
1 tablespoon thyme leaves
60 g/1 cup grated Parmesan

Relish
800 g/6 cups (about 2 large) diced aubergine/eggplant
125 ml/½ cup red wine
250 ml/1 cup balsamic vinegar
½ star anise
1 tablespoon caster/granulated sugar
125 ml/½ cup sunflower oil
1 tablespoon currants
3 tablespoons pine nuts/kernels, toasted
2 tablespoons chopped flat-leaf parsley
salt

6 x 250-ml/1-cup capacity ramekins, greased

SERVES 6

Preheat the oven to 200°C (400°F) Gas 6.

Drain the ricotta in a fine mesh sieve/strainer and put in a large mixing bowl. Pound the garlic with the salt in a pestle and mortar. Stir the garlic paste through the ricotta together with the egg yolks, lemon zest, thyme and grated Parmesan.

In a separate large mixing bowl, whisk the egg whites to soft peaks.

Add a large spoonful of the egg whites to the ricotta mixture and stir to loosen it. Gently fold in the remaining egg whites until just incorporated, then pour the mixture into the prepared ramekins.

Bake in the preheated oven for 20 minutes, until slightly golden on top and the cheese is just set. It will puff up slightly during cooking and deflate while cooling, so don't be alarmed. Allow the ricotta to cool completely before turning out onto serving plates.

Next, make the relish. Put the aubergine/eggplant in a large sieve/strainer set over a mixing bowl, cover with salt and set aside for 20 minutes. Rinse, pat dry and set aside. Place the red wine, balsamic vinegar, star anise and sugar in a medium saucepan or pot set over medium heat. Bring to the boil, then reduce the heat and simmer for about 15 minutes, until the liquid has reduced by two-thirds and become syrupy.

Meanwhile, heat the oil in a large frying pan/skillet over a medium heat. Shallow fry the aubergine/eggplant in batches until golden brown. Add extra oil as required. Drain the aubergine/eggplant on paper towels and set aside.

Remove the star anise from the red wine reduction. Add the currants and fried aubergine/eggplant, and simmer gently over low heat with a lid on for 30 minutes – most of the liquid should be soaked up. Remove from the heat and stir in the pine nuts/kernels and parsley.

Season to taste and serve with the baked ricotta.

Ricotta and spinach dumplings with cherry tomato sauce

Inspired by Italian cuisine, this recipe uses ricotta, together with spinach, to make little dumplings. The sauce here is a simple tomato one, flavoured with basil, lemon and a touch of chilli/chile for a hint of piquancy.

400 g/14 oz. fresh spinach
250 g/1 cup ricotta
2 eggs
100 g/¾ cup fine
    semolina, plus extra
    for coating
50 g/⅔ cup grated
    Parmesan, plus extra
    for serving
freshly grated nutmeg
butter, for greasing
salt and freshly ground
    black pepper

Sauce
2 tablespoons olive oil
2 garlic cloves, chopped
a splash of dry white wine
    (optional)
2 x 395-g/14-oz. cans of
    peeled cherry tomatoes
2 pinches of dried chilli/
    hot red pepper flakes or
    1 peperoncino,
    crumbled
a generous handful of
    fresh basil leaves
a sprinkle of freshly
    grated lemon zest

*an ovenproof serving dish,
    generously buttered*

SERVES 4

Rinse the spinach well, discarding any discoloured or wilted leaves. Place it in a large, heavy-based saucepan and cook, covered, over medium heat until the spinach has just wilted, so that it retains some texture. Strain in a colander, pressing out any excess moisture and set it aside to cool. Once cooled, chop the spinach finely, again squeezing out any excess moisture.

While the spinach is cooling, place the ricotta in a clean kitchen cloth in a sieve/strainer over a bowl to drain off any excess moisture.

For the cherry tomato sauce, heat the olive oil in a heavy-based frying pan/skillet. Add the garlic and fry, stirring, until golden brown. Add the white wine and cook, stirring, until it has largely evaporated. Add the cherry tomatoes, chilli/hot red pepper flakes and lemon zest. Roughly tear the basil (reserving a few leaves) and mix in. Season with salt and pepper. Cook, uncovered, for 5–10 minutes, stirring now and then until the sauce has thickened.

Place the ricotta in a large bowl and break it up with a fork. Mix in the finely chopped spinach thoroughly. Add the eggs, semolina and Parmesan and mix well. Season with salt, pepper and nutmeg and mix again.

Sprinkle semolina on a large plate. Take a teaspoon of the ricotta mixture and, using a second teaspoon, shape it into a little nugget. Still using teaspoons, place this ricotta dumpling on the semolina and roll, lightly coating it. Repeat the process until all the ricotta has been shaped into dumplings.

Preheat the oven to 190°C (350°F) Gas 5, and while it's preheating, gently reheat the cherry tomato sauce. Place the buttered serving dish in the oven to warm through. Line a plate with paper towels.

Bring a large saucepan of salted water to the boil. Cook the dumplings in batches, adding them to the boiling water a few at a time – you shouldn't over-crowd the pan. Cook over medium heat until they float to the surface, around 2–3 minutes. Remove the dumplings using a shallow, slotted spoon, drain on the paper-lined plate, then carefully transfer to the serving dish in the oven to keep warm. Repeat the process until all the dumplings have been cooked.

Tear the remaining basil leaves and stir into the cherry tomato sauce. Serve the dumplings with the sauce and extra Parmesan on the side.

Stuffed giant mushrooms with feta and herbs

8 very large mushrooms, stalks removed

100 g/½ cup feta, crumbled

40 g/⅓ cup blanched almonds, roughly chopped

50 g/⅔ cup stale white breadcrumbs

1 tablespoon chopped fresh flat leaf parsley

1 tablespoon snipped fresh chives

2 teaspoons olive oil

1 tablespoon chilled butter, finely cubed, plus 2 tablespoons extra

6 baby courgettes/ zucchini, halved lengthways

100 g/3½ oz. fine green beans, trimmed

4 small leeks, thinly sliced

65 ml/4 tablespoons dry white wine

freshly squeezed lemon juice, to taste

sea salt flakes and freshly ground black pepper

an ovenproof baking dish, lightly oiled

SERVES 4

Look out for pine mushrooms in the autumn. They will be foraged and hand-picked by specialists. Cook them whole with as little fuss as possible; their flavour is best appreciated if they are left to sit for a short while then served warm rather than hot.

Preheat the oven to 170°C (325°F) Gas 3.

Sit the mushrooms, gill-side up, in the prepared baking dish. Put the feta, almonds, breadcrumbs and herbs in a bowl and use your fingers to quickly combine. Stir in the olive oil. Spoon the mixture into the mushrooms and press down gently. Dot the cubed butter over the top. Bake in the preheated oven for about 40–45 minutes, until the mushrooms are really soft and the tops golden.

Meanwhile, bring a saucepan of lightly salted water to the boil. Add the courgettes/zucchini and beans to the water and cook for 1 minute. Drain well and set aside. About 15 minutes before the mushrooms are cooked, heat the extra butter in a frying pan/skillet set over high heat. Add the leeks and cook for 2 minutes, stirring until softened. Add the courgettes/zucchini and beans and cook for 2–3 minutes, until tender. Add the wine and cook for 1 minute further, until almost all of it has evaporated. Add a squeeze of lemon juice and season well with sea salt and freshly ground black pepper.

Arrange the vegetables on a serving plate and sit the mushrooms on top.

Sweet and sour bell peppers with mozzarella

6 (bell) peppers, a mixture of red, yellow and orange

3 tablespoons white wine vinegar

6 tablespoons fruity extra virgin olive oil

50 g/⅓ cup sultanas/ golden raisins

1½ teaspoons cumin seeds

1 teaspoon crushed dried peperoncini chillies/ chiles

sea salt flakes and freshly ground black pepper

1 garlic clove, finely sliced

2 teaspoons caster/ granulated sugar

Salad

3 x 125-g/4½-oz. balls buffalo mozzarella, sliced

6 large green olives, pitted/stoned and sliced lengthways

60 g/2¼ oz. rocket/ arugula

1 tablespoon extra virgin olive oil, light and not too bold

crusty bread, to serve

a baking sheet lined with baking parchment

SERVES 4–6

This antipasto is timeless and its colour, simplicity and flavour always hit the right key. It is ideal for those with busy lives, as it can be made days in advance. Any leftover roasted (bell) peppers make a wonderful snack with bread to dip into the juice.

Preheat the oven to 200°C (400°F) Gas 6.

Place the (bell) peppers on the prepared baking sheet and bake for 25 minutes until slightly blackened and deflated. Leave to cool. Peel the (bell) peppers and discard the seeds, then cut into 1-cm/½-in. strips.

Mix the (bell) pepper strips with the vinegar, oil, sultanas/golden raisins, cumin and peperoncini chillies/chiles. Season to taste. Add the garlic and sugar and set aside to infuse.

To serve, divide the mozzarella between 4–6 plates, spoon over the (bell) pepper mixture and scatter over the olives. Toss the rocket/arugula leaves in the oil and scatter some on each plate. Serve immediately with crusty bread.

Salads and Soups

When fruit and cheese are paired with leaves, they combine to create a salad that is far more of a treat than a chore. In this chapter try grapefruit with feta, Roquefort and apple or halloumi with pomegranate. Or how about a warming soup with all the goodness of vegetables, but naughty swirls of molten cheese to sweeten the deal.

Watermelon and ricotta salata salad with olive salt

This is a delightfully pretty and refreshing salad in which the olive salt brings out the sweetness of the watermelon. Ricotta salata, a lightly salted cheese made from sheep's milk, originates from the island of Sicily. If you can't find a mini watermelon, buy the smallest available and cut it in half. You can use feta cheese if ricotta salata isn't available.

1 mini seedless watermelon
170 g/1½ cups ricotta salata, or feta
2 tablespoons fresh oregano leaves
olive oil, to drizzle
freshly ground black pepper

Olive salt
10 black olives, pitted/stoned
2½ tablespoons sea salt flakes

SERVES 2

Peel the watermelon and cut it into bite-sized chunks. Put in a serving bowl, crumble the ricotta salata over the watermelon and sprinkle with the oregano.

To make the Olive Salt, chop the olives roughly. Grind them with the salt using a pestle and mortar until the olives are mashed.

Drizzle the olive oil over the salad and season with black pepper. Sprinkle with a generous amount of the olive salt. Put the remainder of the salt in a bowl to use on other dishes.

Roquefort, pecan and apple salad

Apple and cheese are natural partners. Here, the apples are pan-fried in a light honey–butter sauce until golden and glossy, while the piquant blue cheese balances out any sweetness.

30 g/1 tablespoon butter
2 large, crisp eating apples, peeled, cored, and each apple cut into 10 wedges
1 tablespoon clear honey
100 g/3¾ oz. watercress, tough stalks removed
50 g/2 oz. baby spinach leaves, tough stalks discarded
175 g/6 oz. Roquefort or other blue cheese, crumbled into chunks
60 g/½ cup pecan halves, toasted

Dressing
5 tablespoons extra virgin olive oil
2 tablespoons apple cider vinegar
1 teaspoon Dijon mustard
sea salt flakes and freshly ground black pepper

SERVES 4

Mix together all the ingredients for the dressing and season lightly with salt, bearing in mind that Roquefort is already quite salty, and more generously with pepper.

Melt the butter in a large, non-stick frying pan/skillet. Add the apple wedges and cook for 5 minutes, turning once. Stir in the honey, turn the apples to coat them in the honey-butter sauce and cook for 1 minute more, or until golden and glossy. Remove from the pan and set aside.

Spoon as much of the dressing over the watercress and spinach as needed to coat the leaves in a serving bowl. Toss until combined, then top with the apples, Roquefort and pecans. Serve immediately.

Puy lentils, grapefruit and feta with harissa dressing

Harissa, the fiery North African spice paste, adds both colour and flavour to the dressing for this substantial Puy lentil salad. Oranges can be substituted for the grapefruit, if you prefer a slightly sweeter fruit. Serve with warm flatbread on the side.

250 g/9 oz. dried Puy
  lentils
60 g/2 oz. watercress,
  tough stalks removed,
  separated into small
  sprigs
60 g/2 oz. baby spinach
  leaves, tough stalks
  trimmed
1 pink or red grapefruit,
  peeled, pith removed
  and segmented
1 small red onion, diced
a handful of mixed
  sprouted beans
200 g/7 oz. feta, cubed

Dressing
5 tablespoons extra virgin
  olive oil
3 tablespoons freshly
  squeezed orange juice
1 teaspoon harissa paste
sea salt flakes and freshly
  ground black pepper

SERVES 4

Put the lentils in a pan and cover with plenty of water. Bring to the boil, then turn the heat down and simmer, part-covered, for 25 minutes or until tender. Drain and transfer the lentils to a serving bowl.

Meanwhile, mix together all the ingredients for the dressing, season and set aside.

Add the watercress and spinach to the serving bowl. Remove the membrane from the grapefruit segments over a dish and add the segments to the salad. Pour any juice from the grapefruit into the dressing.

Add the onion and mixed bean sprouts and pour the dressing over. Toss the salad until thoroughly combined and sprinkle the feta over before serving.

Pecorino, olive and parsley salad

½ round/butterhead
  lettuce, leaves
  separated
6 large handfuls of freshly
  chopped flat leaf
  parsley
100 g/3¾ oz. pitted/
  stoned black olives,
  drained and thinly
  sliced into rounds
6 sundried tomatoes,
  finely chopped
3 celery sticks, finely
  chopped
3 spring onions/scallions,
  finely chopped
60 g/2¼ oz. pecorino,
  sliced into thin
  shavings

Dressing
4 tablespoons extra virgin
  olive oil
finely grated zest and
  freshly squeezed juice
  of 1 lemon
2 teaspoons red wine
  vinegar
1 small garlic clove,
  crushed
sea salt flakes and freshly
  ground black pepper

SERVES 4

Fresh and vibrant, this robust salad makes an excellent accompaniment to fish, meat or egg dishes, and it's also good served on top of bruschetta or stirred into pasta, rice or beans. Pecorino works well, but so would a crumbly goat's cheese or a creamy burrata.

Arrange the lettuce leaves in a salad bowl. Combine the parsley, olives, sundried tomatoes, celery and spring onions/scallions in a separate bowl.

Mix together all the ingredients for the dressing and season. Pour enough of the dressing over the parsley mixture to coat, and toss until combined. Spoon the mixture on top of the lettuce leaves, then sprinkle the pecorino shavings over before serving.

Chargrilled halloumi and mint salad

125 g/4 oz. rocket/arugula leaves

600 g/1lb. 5 oz. canned chickpeas, drained and rinsed

1 small red onion, sliced

1 courgette/zucchini, coarsely grated

400-g/14-oz. halloumi, patted dry and sliced

seeds from ½ pomegranate

4 tablespoons freshly chopped mint leaves

Dressing

4 tablespoons extra virgin olive oil, plus extra for brushing

2 tablespoons pomegranate molasses

1 teaspoon freshly squeezed lemon juice

½ teaspoon caster/superfine sugar

sea salt flakes and freshly ground black pepper

SERVES 4

Pomegranate molasses, a popular ingredient in Middle Eastern cooking, lends a tangy, sweet-sour flavour to the dressing for this main meal salad. It also makes a useful marinade base and goes particularly well with bean, poultry, meat and vegetable dishes.

Mix together all the ingredients for the dressing and season with salt and pepper.

Divide the rocket/arugula, chickpeas, red onion and courgette/zucchini between 4 serving plates. Spoon enough of the dressing over the salad to lightly coat it and toss gently until everything is combined.

Heat a large, ridged griddle pan over high heat. Brush the halloumi slices with a little extra olive oil. Reduce the heat a little and griddle the halloumi for 2 minutes on each side or until slightly blackened in places and softened. Serve the halloumi on top of the salad, garnished with the pomegranate seeds and mint.

Provolone, pear and walnut salad

Provolone is a cow's milk cheese from Italy's southern region. It has a slightly smoky flavour and fine texture. The colour is pale yellow when aged between 2 and 3 months, but as the cheese ripens, the colour and flavour deepen. A mature goat's cheese would also work very well.

100 g/1 cup fresh walnut halves
1 head chicory/endive
½ head radicchio
a handful of fresh basil, torn
2 tablespoons freshly chopped mint leaves
125 g/4½ oz. pea shoots
2 large, ripe but firm pears (Williams are good)
150 g/5½ oz. Provolone, cut into triangles

Vinaigrette
1 tablespoon red wine vinegar
2 teaspoons aged balsamic vinegar
3 tablespoons walnut oil
1 tablespoon olive oil
sea salt flakes and freshly ground black pepper

SERVES 4–6

Preheat the oven to 180°C (350°F) Gas 4.

Spread the walnuts on a baking sheet and bake them for 10 minutes until fragrant. Let cool before roughly chopping.

Next, make the vinaigrette. Combine the salt, red wine vinegar and balsamic vinegar in a bowl and whisk until the salt has dissolved. Trickle in the two types of oil, whisking all the while until the mixture has emulsified. Season to taste with freshly ground pepper.

Separate the chicory/endive and radicchio leaves, rinse well and pat dry. Place in a bowl with the herbs and pea shoots. Add 2 tablespoons of the vinaigrette and toss well, then use to make a bed on a plate.

Quarter and core the pears, then arrange them on top of the leaves with the cheese and walnuts. Drizzle with the dressing and serve straight away.

Sun-blush tomato, orange and burrata salad

Gloriously simple to put together, this bright and colourful dish offers a Mediterranean-inspired combination of colours, textures and flavours.

2 large oranges
24 sun-blush/semi-dried cherry tomato halves
2 burrata cheeses (or good-quality fresh mozzarella cheese)

To serve
extra virgin olive oil
freshly ground black pepper
a handful of fresh basil leaves

SERVES 4

Peel the oranges, making sure to trim off all the white pith, and cut into thick, even slices.

Place the orange slices on a large serving dish, then scatter over the sun-blush/semi-dried tomato halves. Tear the burrata cheeses into chunks and layer on top of the orange slices.

Drizzle with extra virgin olive oil and season with pepper. Garnish with basil leaves and serve at once.

Paneer with warm curried lentil salad and a spiced dressing

This fresh and tasty salad is mildly spiced and perfect with the fried paneer. The salad itself keeps well so can be made in advance, allowing the flavours to develop.

400-g/14-oz. can green lentils
2 celery sticks, finely sliced
2 carrots, grated
50 g/heaped ⅓ cup cashews, toasted
½ mango, cut in half and sliced lengthways
finely grated zest of ½ a lime
1 tablespoon vegetable oil
200 g/7 oz. paneer, sliced
a handful of fresh mint or coriander/cilantro leaves, chopped
lime wedges, to serve

Dressing
4 tablespoons vegetable oil
1 shallot, finely chopped
½ teaspoon mustard seeds
1 teaspoon garam masala
½ teaspoon turmeric
a pinch of dried chilli/hot red pepper flakes
1 garlic clove, crushed
1 teaspoon sugar
1 tablespoon white wine vinegar
50 g/⅓ cup sultanas/ golden raisins
½ fresh red chilli/chile, deseeded and finely diced

SERVES 2–4

To make the spiced dressing, heat half the oil in a small saucepan. Add the shallot and cook over low heat for 5 minutes, until it starts to soften but still has a slight bite and has not taken on any colour. Add the remaining oil, mustard seeds, garam masala, turmeric, dried chilli/hot red pepper flakes, garlic and sugar, and cook for 2 minutes. Turn off the heat and add the vinegar, sultanas and fresh chilli/chile.

For the salad, put the lentils, celery, carrots, toasted cashews, mango and lime zest in a large bowl. Pour in the warm dressing, reserving about 2 tablespoons to serve, and stir until well combined and coated in the dressing.

To cook the paneer, heat the oil in a frying pan/skillet and fry the slices until golden on both sides, using tongs to turn half way through cooking.

Brush the paneer slices with the reserved dressing and serve with the salad. Finish the salad with fresh mint or coriander/cilantro, and with lime wedges on the side for squeezing.

Warm pearl barley, smoked Cheddar and walnut salad

A rustic, warming, wintry dish, this salad is both hearty and sustaining. Pearl barley has a slightly chewy texture when cooked and goes well with strong flavours, such as the rosemary, garlic and smoked Cheddar cheese in this recipe. The salad is also good topped with shards of crispy bacon.

200 g/7 oz. pearl barley, rinsed
60 g/½ cup walnut pieces
2 tablespoons olive oil
1 large onion, chopped
3 garlic cloves, finely chopped
1 tablespoon freshly chopped rosemary
400 g/14 oz. baby spinach leaves, sliced
2 handfuls of freshly chopped flat leaf parsley
100 g/3¾ oz. smoked Cheddar, cubed

Dressing
2 tablespoons extra virgin olive oil
1 heaped teaspoon wholegrain mustard
1 heaped teaspoon clear honey
freshly squeezed juice of 1 lemon
sea salt flakes and freshly ground black pepper

SERVES 4

Put the barley in a medium-sized pan and cover generously with water. Bring to the boil, then turn the heat down and simmer, part-covered, for 30 minutes or until tender. Drain and set aside.

Meanwhile, toast the walnuts in a large, dry sauté pan for 4 minutes, turning occasionally, until they smell toasted and start to colour. Transfer to a bowl and leave to cool.

Add the olive oil to the sauté pan and fry the onion for 6 minutes, stirring regularly, until softened. Add the garlic, rosemary and spinach, and cook for another 3 minutes, turning the leaves with tongs, until the spinach has wilted.

Meanwhile, mix all the ingredients for the dressing together until combined, and season with salt and pepper.

Transfer the barley to a serving bowl with the spinach mixture and parsley. Pour the dressing over and toss until combined. Add the Cheddar cubes and toss again, then serve, sprinkled with the walnuts.

Brie, bean and crispy caper salad

1 tablespoon olive oil

6 tablespoons capers, drained, rinsed and patted dry

300 g/11 oz. drained canned butter/lima beans, rinsed

6 vine-ripened tomatoes, quartered, seeded and chopped

100 g/3¾ oz. rocket/arugula leaves

40 g/1½ oz. pea shoots

200 g/7 oz. just-ripe Brie, sliced

Dressing

5 tablespoons extra virgin olive oil

1 large garlic clove, peeled and halved

2 tablespoons white wine vinegar

1 teaspoon wholegrain mustard

4 tablespoons chopped fresh flat leaf parsley

sea salt flakes and freshly ground black pepper

SERVES 4

The Brie is best when just ripe so it's soft and oozy without being too runny. Crisp, salty and piquant, the capers take on a new dimension when fried in olive oil; and along with the Brie, they certainly give this delicious bean salad a lift. Serve simply with crusty bread.

Heat the oil in a large frying pan/skillet over a medium heat and fry the capers for 3–5 minutes or until crisp and starting to colour; take care as they can splutter. Drain on paper towels and leave to cool.

Meanwhile, start to make the dressing. Gently heat the extra virgin olive oil and the garlic in a small pan for 2 minutes. Take the pan off the heat and leave to infuse.

Tip the butter/lima beans into a large serving bowl and add the tomatoes, rocket/arugula and pea shoots.

Remove the garlic from the oil and pour it into a jug/pitcher. Whisk in the vinegar, mustard and parsley. Season, bearing in mind that the capers are salty, and pour the dressing over the salad. Toss to coat the salad in the dressing, and top with the Brie slices and capers.

Ossau iraty, asparagus and crouton salad

Ossau iraty is a French semi-hard sheep's cheese with a nutty taste and creamy texture that complements the earthy beetroot/beets. Use Parmesan, Gruyère or Emmental, if you prefer.

4 thick slices country-style bread, roughly torn into croutons

3 tablespoons olive oil

400 g/14 oz. asparagus spears, ends trimmed

150 g/5 oz. mixed baby salad leaves

4 raw chioggia or red beetroot/beets, cut into paper-thin round slices

100 g/3¾ oz. ossau iraty, thinly sliced into shavings

Dressing

6 tablespoons extra virgin olive oil

freshly squeezed juice of ½ small lemon

freshly squeezed juice of ½ small orange

1 teaspoon Dijon mustard

1 garlic clove, peeled and halved

salt and freshly ground black pepper

SERVES 4

Preheat the oven to 200°C (400°F) Gas 6.

While the oven is heating, put all the ingredients for the dressing in a small jar, season and shake until combined. Set aside.

Put the croutons in a small food bag and add 2 tablespoons of the oil. Shake the bag until the croutons are coated in the oil. Spread the croutons out evenly in a large roasting pan and toast in the preheated oven for 15 minutes, turning once, until golden and crisp.

Brush the remaining oil over the asparagus and season with salt and pepper. Arrange the asparagus in a separate roasting pan and roast, turning once, for 10 minutes until tender and just starting to colour.

Meanwhile, arrange the salad leaves in four serving bowls. Top with the beetroot/beets and asparagus, then spoon enough of the dressing over to coat and toss gently until combined. Sprinkle the ossau iraty shavings and toasted croutons over before serving.

French onion soup with Gruyère garlic toasts

Richly flavoured beef stock and tangy Gruyère cheese make this soup a thing of beauty. There aren't many other ingredients, so it follows that there aren't many places for mistakes to hide. Therefore you need to nail the caramelization of the onions – cook them slowly at first, then turn up the heat and cook until sticky and golden brown.

50 g/3½ tablespoons butter
1 kg/2¼ lb. onions, sliced
2 garlic cloves, crushed
1 tablespoon caster/superfine sugar
2 tablespoons Cognac or brandy
300 ml/10½ fl oz. dry cider
1.2 litres/5 cups beef stock
1 bouquet garni (1 sprig each of parsley, thyme and bay)
sea salt flakes and freshly ground black pepper

Garlic toasts
4 tablespoons extra virgin olive oil
1 garlic clove, crushed
1 small baguette or ½ large baguette, sliced
200 g/2 packed cups grated Gruyère

SERVES 4

Preheat the oven to 180°C (350°F) Gas 4.

To make the garlic toasts, mix the olive oil and garlic together and season well. Arrange the baguette slices on a baking sheet and brush with the garlic oil. Bake in the preheated oven for 25 minutes until crisp.

Melt the butter in a large saucepan or casserole over medium heat. Add the onions and garlic and stir until starting to soften. Turn the heat to low, cover and cook gently for 25–30 minutes until really softened.

Take the lid off and add the sugar. Cook for a further 20 minutes, stirring until golden brown and extremely floppy-looking. This is the secret to a successful onion soup. Pour in the Cognac and cider and leave to bubble up for 1 minute. Add the stock and bouquet garni and stir to blend. Simmer for 45 minutes, then season to taste. Remove the bouquet garni.

Preheat the grill/broiler.

Divide the soup between 4 ovenproof bowls and place them on a baking sheet. Float 2–3 garlic toasts on top of each bowl and scatter the Gruyère over the toasts. Grill/broil until the Gruyère is bubbling and golden. Remove the baking sheet and lift off the hot bowls with an oven glove, warning everyone that they are hot.

Spinach and Parmesan soup with nutmeg and rosemary

50 g/3½ tablespoons
  butter
6 strong shallots,
  chopped
2 garlic cloves, crushed
1 large potato, peeled and
  diced
2 tablespoons chopped
  fresh rosemary leaves,
  plus extra sprigs to
  garnish
1.5 litres/6 cups chicken
  stock
1 kg/2¼ lbs. spinach
  leaves, any really coarse
  stalks removed and
  chopped to a
  manageable size
a pinch of grated nutmeg,
  plus extra to garnish
200 g/2 cups freshly
  grated Parmesan, or
  other hard strong
  cheese
a few tablespoons of
  crème fraîche or sour
  cream, to taste
sea salt flakes and freshly
  ground black pepper

SERVES 6–8

This soup calls for a robust cheese, such as Parmesan, but any other hard, strong cheese would do. The trick, as with so many recipes, is to keep the ingredients in the same company as if they were like-minded people – it makes for a much more harmonious party. To go with the fresh rosemary you can use the tender, washed bags of spinach found in supermarkets/stores or a tougher variety such as epinard, with the tough stalks trimmed.

In a large saucepan, melt the butter and gently cook the shallots with the garlic for a few minutes, until softened. Add the potato and rosemary, cover with the stock and bring to a simmer. Cook for 15–20 minutes, until the potato is tender.

Add the spinach to the pan and bring to the boil, then draw the pan off the heat and blend everything well with a stick blender. Add a grating of nutmeg, to taste, and season well with salt and pepper. Stir in the Parmesan and most of the crème fraîche, to enrich the soup.

Ladle the soup into bowls and serve garnished with a dusting of nutmeg, a spoonful of the remaining crème fraîche and sprigs of fresh rosemary.

Purple sprouting broccoli soup with Mrs Bells Blue

Judy Bell of Shepherds Purse Cheeses has been a pioneer in cheese-making in the UK, and Mrs Bells Blue, a soft blue sheep's-milk cheese is one of her best. If it is unavailable, you can use any not-too-strong blue cheese, such as Stilton. Use the purple sprouting variety of broccoli for making soup, when available, as the colour and flavour is superior and more intense.

50 g/3½ tablespoons butter
6 banana shallots, finely chopped
3 potatoes, peeled and diced
4 celery sticks, sliced
1.5 litres/6 cups chicken stock
950 g/2 lbs. 2 oz. purple sprouting or new-season tender broccoli
400 g/14 oz. Mrs Bells Blue or other creamy blue cheese, eg. Stilton
a pinch of grated nutmeg
200 ml/¾ cup double/heavy cream
freshly ground black pepper
croutons, to serve

SERVES 6

Melt the butter in a large saucepan, add the shallots and cook gently for a few minutes to soften. Add the potato and celery, and stir to coat well with the butter. Add the stock and bring the liquid to the boil, then simmer for 15–20 minutes, until the potato is almost tender.

Add the broccoli and continue to cook for a further 3–5 minutes, until the stalks are tender. It is crucial not to overcook the broccoli or you lose the lovely bright green colour. Purée the soup immediately with a stick blender.

When smooth, crumble in three-quarters of the blue cheese and add a pinch of nutmeg and a good twist of black pepper, to season. (The cheese can be quite salty, so you probably won't need salt, too.) Stir in almost all of the cream, reserving a little to garnish.

Ladle the soup into bowls, garnish with a swirl of cream and crumble over the remaining blue cheese. Serve piping hot as quickly as possible, with croutons.

Pear, celery and blue cheese soup with salted sugared walnuts

60 g/4 tablespoons butter
6 shallots, diced
1 leek, white only, sliced
1 large potato, peeled and diced
½ celeriac/celery root, peeled and diced
1.5 litres/6 cups vegetable stock
6 celery sticks, sliced
2 large pears (hard ones are best for this as less grainy), peeled, cored and roughly diced
400 g/14 oz. blue cheese (Stilton, dolcelatte or similar), crumbled
a small bunch of fresh flat leaf parsley, chopped
2 tablespoons double/heavy cream
freshly ground black pepper
baby rocket/arugula leaves, to serve

Salted walnuts
½ teaspoon rock salt
1 teaspoon caster/superfine sugar
a handful of shelled walnuts

a baking sheet, lined with parchment paper

SERVES 6–8

This soup is rather 'old school', but the addition of the walnuts and rocket/arugula bring it up to date! This is delicious, and great to use up any leftover Stilton, especially accompanied by a shot of sloe gin.

Melt the butter in a large saucepan and add the shallots, leek, potato and celeriac/celery root. Sauté until just softened and the butter is absorbed, then cover with the stock and add the celery. Simmer for about 15–20 minutes, until all the vegetables are tender, then toss in the pears and most of the blue cheese, reserving a little to garnish. Simmer for a further 3 minutes or so, until the pears are softened, then draw the pan off the heat and blend well with a stick blender until smooth. Stir in the chopped parsley, season with black pepper and stir in the cream to enrich the soup.

To make the salted walnut garnish, preheat the oven to 180°C (350°F) Gas 4.

Combine the rock salt and sugar in a pestle and mortar and pound until the salt is ground down to a powder. Put the walnuts in a plastic bag with the salt-and-sugar powder and shake to coat them. Sprinkle the coated nuts onto the prepared baking sheet and toast in the preheated oven for 10–15 minutes until slightly darkened, but do not burn. Leave to cool and as they do they will crisp up.

Serve the soup in rustic bowls, garnished with the salted walnuts, the remaining blue cheese and rocket/arugula leaves.

Tomato and red bell pepper soup with Wensleydale

Wensleydale cheese is made in the heart of the English countryside, and its texture is unique. It really is the very best cheese for this soup – its lovely creamy but tangy flavour and springy texture contrasts perfectly with the sweet tomato and red (bell) pepper base. If you can't find Wensleydale, a not-too-salty feta would be the next best choice. This soup is wonderfully versatile and can be used as a base for a pasta sauce or chilli, too. Enjoy it as it is, or experiment to make it your own.

2 tablespoons olive oil, plus extra for drizzling
1 small onion, diced
1 garlic clove, crushed
1 red (bell) pepper, deseeded and diced
700 g/1 lb. 9 oz. fresh tomatoes, finely chopped, or canned chopped tomatoes
800 ml/3⅓ cups vegetable stock
a pinch of paprika
a few sprigs of fresh basil, plus a few extra leaves to garnish
90 g/6 tablespoons tomato purée/paste
sea salt flakes and freshly ground black pepper
reduced balsamic vinegar, for drizzling
250 g/9 oz. Wensleydale, diced, to serve

SERVES 6

Heat the olive oil in a large saucepan, add the onion, garlic and red (bell) pepper and cook for a few minutes, until softened. Add all but 120 g/4 oz. of the tomatoes and pour over the stock. Stir in a pinch of paprika – not too much, as this is just to give a little warmth, not any great heat! – and add the basil. Cover and simmer for about 15 minutes.

Draw the pan off the heat and blend with a stick blender until smooth, then add the reserved chopped tomato and the tomato purée/paste. Cook for a few more minutes to warm the tomatoes through, then season with salt and black pepper.

Ladle the soup into warmed soup bowls and scatter cubes of Wensleydale cheese over the soup, along with a few leaves of fresh basil. Drizzle with a little olive oil and a few drops of reduced balsamic vinegar for a dramatic finish.

Quiches, Tarts and Pies

Cheese and pastry are together one of life's greatest pleasures. Whether you want something that is stylish and light such as the Asparagus, Goat's Cheese and Spinach Tart, or homely and comforting like the Ricotta, Sausage and Potato Pizza Pie, you will find a little of what you fancy here. Choose a pie with store-bought filo/phyllo or puff pastry for a speedy option, or go the extra mile and make a shortcrust pastry from scratch.

Butternut squash, feta and sage quiche

A basic quiche recipe is a useful thing to have in your cooking repertoire. There are many combinations of vegetables, cheeses and herbs that work well so this recipe can be adapted to suit your chosen ingredients.

Pastry

225 g/1¾ cups plain/
   all-purpose flour

a pinch of salt

130 g/1 stick plus 1
   tablespoon cold butter,
   diced

1 egg yolk mixed with 2
   tablespoons milk

Filling

180 g/a good ¾ cup
   double/heavy cream

3 large eggs

1 teaspoon Dijon mustard

30 g/scant ½ cup grated
   Parmesan (optional)

1 butternut squash,
   peeled, deseeded and
   chopped

2 tablespoons olive oil

80 g/⅔ cup crumbled feta

1 teaspoon fresh sage
   leaves, finely chopped

salt and freshly ground
   black pepper

a 23-cm/9-in. tart pan
baking beans

SERVES 4–6

Preheat the oven to 190°C (375°F) Gas 5.

Rub the butter into the flour using your fingertips until the mixture looks like breadcrumbs. Sprinkle the pastry with 1½ tablespoons of the egg and milk mixture, stirring it through with a knife. Use your hands to lightly bring the dough together in the bowl but do not knead it. If the dough still feels dry, add another ½ tablespoon of the egg and milk mixture. Continue until you can bring the dough together into a smooth, firm dough.

Roll out on a lightly floured work surface, or between 2 sheets of baking parchment, until it is about 3 mm/⅛ in. thick. Use your rolling pin to pick up the dough and lay it over the tart pan. Gently push the dough down into the pan, making sure that the base and edges are well lined. Roll a rolling pin over the top of the tart pan to remove any excess dough and tidy the edges with your fingertips. Chill the tart shell in the refrigerator for 30 minutes until firm.

Lay a round of baking parchment slightly bigger than the tart pan over the tart shell, pushing the paper down onto the base. Fill with baking beans and bake in the top of the preheated oven for 15 minutes. After 15 minutes, remove the parchment and baking beans and put the tart shell back in the preheated oven for a further 5 minutes, until there are no grey patches and the surface of the pastry has a sandy feel.

Meanwhile, make the custard, put all the ingredients in a bowl and beat together until well mixed. Strain the mixture for a smooth custard.

Put the hot oven up to 200°C (400°F) Gas 6.

To make the filling, lay the squash in a roasting pan and drizzle with olive oil, and add salt and pepper, to taste. Roast the squash for 30 minutes, until it turns soft and starts to brown. Allow to cool, then stir it through the custard mixture, along with the feta and sage. Spoon the filling into the tart shell. Bake in the middle of the oven for around 20 minutes, until the custard is just set but has a slight, even wobble towards the centre if you gently shake the pan. Serve at room temperature with a green salad.

Swiss chard, ricotta and pine nut/kernel tart

Ricotta gives this delicately flavoured tart an appealing lightness. Serve it with little gem lettuce leaves and a creamy dressing topped with chopped chives.

50 g/½ cup pine nuts/
   kernels
300 g/10 oz. prepared
   shortcrust pastry
   dough
300 g/10 oz. Swiss chard
2 medium shallots
2 teaspoons olive oil
1 teaspoon balsamic
   vinegar
2 eggs, beaten
300 ml/1¼ cups crème
   fraîche or sour cream
50 g/⅔ cup grated
   Parmesan
salt and freshly ground
   black pepper
freshly grated nutmeg
250 g/1 cup ricotta,
   drained in a sieve/
   strainer to remove
   excess moisture

a 24-cm/9½-in. tart pan
baking beans

SERVES 6

Preheat the oven to 200°C (400°F) Gas 6.

Firstly, dry-fry the pine nuts/kernels in a small frying pan/skillet over a medium heat. Shake the pan every 20 seconds to avoid burning them. Remove them when they're golden on both sides, then set them aside.

Next, make the pastry case. Roll out the pastry dough on a lightly floured work surface. Use the pastry dough to line the tart pan. Press it in firmly and prick the base to stop it from bubbling up as it bakes. Line the case with a piece of baking parchment and fill it with baking beans. Blind bake the pastry case for 15 minutes. Carefully remove the baking beans and parchment and bake for a further 5 minutes.

While the pastry case is baking, prepare the filling. Rinse the Swiss chard, then place it in a heavy-based saucepan, cover and cook over medium heat, stirring now and then, until wilted.

Drain the chard well using a colander, squeeze dry and roughly chop.

Peel the shallots, halve lengthways and halve again crossways. Heat the olive oil in a separate small frying pan/skillet. Fry the shallots gently until softened, then mix in the balsamic vinegar and stir for 1–2 minutes until the shallots are glazed. Set aside to cool.

Lightly whisk together the beaten eggs, crème fraîche and Parmesan. Season with salt and pepper and add the nutmeg.

In the blind-baked pastry case, layer in the glazed shallots, then top with the Swiss chard. Dot the ricotta, in small pieces on top of the Swiss chard and sprinkle over the pine nuts/kernels. Pour in the egg mixture.

Bake for 40 minutes in the preheated oven until golden-brown and puffed up. Serve warm from the oven or at room temperature.

Parmesan, leek and rocket/arugula tart

Almost everyone enjoys a lusciously creamy, freshly baked tart, and while everyone has their own favourite filling, this one tops many a list. The recipe requires a deep pan as there are few things more disappointing than a thin, mean-looking tart.

Pastry
90 g/6 tablespoons cold unsalted butter, cut into small pieces
180 g/1½ cups plain/all-purpose flour
a pinch of sea salt flakes
2–3 tablespoons ice-cold water

Filling
20 g/4 teaspoons butter
2–3 leeks, trimmed and thinly sliced on a diagonal
7 eggs
250 ml/1 cup double/heavy cream
200 g/¾ cup crème fraîche or sour cream
130 g/1⅔ cups grated Parmesan
80 g/1⅓ cup rocket/arugula
sea salt flakes and freshly ground black pepper

a deep 21-cm/8-in. fluted tart pan
baking beans

SERVES 8–10

Preheat the oven to 190°C (375°F) Gas 5.

Place the butter, flour and salt in a food processor and pulse the mixture for 20–30 seconds, until it resembles coarse breadcrumbs. With the motor running, add the ice-cold water slowly and stop as soon as the dough comes together. It is important not to over mix the dough as it will become tough and if you add too much water it will shrink as it cooks. Wrap the dough in clingfilm/plastic wrap and chill in the refrigerator for at least 30 minutes before using.

Roll the dough out as thinly as possible on a lightly floured surface. Line the tart pan with the pastry and prick the base all over with a fork. Place the pan on a baking sheet, line with a piece of greased baking parchment slightly larger than the pan and fill the case with baking beans.

Bake in the preheated oven for 15–20 minutes. Remove the baking beans and parchment and return the pastry case to the oven to cook for a further 5–10 minutes, or until it is pale golden and cooked through. Remove from the oven and set aside to cool.

Reduce the heat to 160°C (325°F) Gas 3.

Melt the butter in a large saucepan or pot set over a medium heat. Add the leeks and sweat until soft but avoid browning.

In a large mixing bowl, whisk together the eggs, cream and crème fraîche. Season with salt and pepper, then gently stir in the Parmesan, cooked leeks and rocket/arugula. Pour the mixture into the cooled tart case, making sure the leeks and rocket/arugula are evenly distributed. Cook for about 1 hour in the still-warm oven, until golden and just set. Serve hot or cold.

Asparagus, goat's cheese and spinach tart

In this tart the asparagus spears float on the surface like synchronised swimmers, and there's no mistaking who's striving to be the star of the show. However the goat's cheese is what gives the filling its main savoury flavour, offsetting the light vegetables perfectly.

Pastry

290 g/6 tablespoons cold unsalted butter, cut into small pieces

180 g/1½ cups plain/all-purpose flour

a pinch of sea salt flakes

2–3 tablespoons ice-cold water

Filling

7 eggs

250 ml/1 cup double/heavy cream

200 g/¾ cup crème fraîche or sour cream

150 g/1½ cups goat's cheese or sour cream

80 g/1⅓ cup baby spinach leaves

12 asparagus spears, ends removed

a deep 21-cm/8-in. fluted tart pan

baking beans

SERVES 8–10

Preheat the oven to 190°C (375°F) Gas 5.

Place the butter, flour and salt in a food processor and pulse the mixture for 20–30 seconds, until it resembles coarse breadcrumbs. With the motor running, add the ice-cold water slowly and stop as soon as the dough comes together. It is important not to over mix the dough as it will become tough and if you add too much water it will shrink as it cooks. Wrap the dough in clingfilm/plastic wrap and chill in the refrigerator for at least 30 minutes.

Roll the dough out as thinly as possible on a lightly floured surface. Line the tart pan with the pastry and prick the base all over with a fork. Place on a baking sheet, line with a piece of greased baking parchment slightly larger than the pan and fill with baking beans.

Bake in the preheated oven for 15–20 minutes. Remove the baking beans and parchment and return the pastry case to the oven to cook for a further 5–10 minutes, or until it is pale golden and cooked through. Remove from the oven and set aside to cool. Reduce the heat to 160°C (325°F) Gas 3.

In a large mixing bowl, whisk together the eggs, cream and crème fraîche. Season with salt and pepper, then gently stir in the goat's cheese and spinach. Pour the mixture into the cooled tart case, making sure the cheese and spinach are evenly distributed.

Lay the asparagus spears in a single layer on top of the egg mixture, alternating heads and tails, and gently push them into the tart. Cook for about 1 hour in the still-warm oven, until golden and just set. Serve hot or cold.

Vegetable and blue cheese tart

The Danes and the Finns each have their own type of blue cheese. It's a popular ingredient in cooking, from salads and pastas to pies. Here's a summer favourite with broccoli and cauliflower, but you can vary the recipe by using your own favourite vegetables – make sure you avoid vegetables that become watery when cooked, or that take a particularly long time to cook.

Pastry
125 g/1 stick plus 1 tablespoon unsalted butter, softened at room temperature
125 g/½ cup quark
125 g/1 scant cup strong white bread flour
½ teaspoon baking powder
a pinch of salt

Filling
200 g/3½–4 cups broccoli florets
200 g/2½ cups cauliflower florets
1 tablespoon rapeseed oil (or vegetable oil)
1 onion, chopped
100 g/8–9 cherry tomatoes, halved
75 g/¾ cup Danish blue cheese, Finnish Aura, or any crumbly blue cheese, crumbled
75 g/1 cup Cheddar, grated
freshly ground black pepper

a 25-cm/10-in. fluted tart pan, greased

SERVES 4–6

To make the pastry put the butter and quark in a mixing bowl and beat together with a wooden spoon until well mixed.

In a separate bowl, mix the flour, baking powder and salt together. Tip into the mixing bowl and mix until a dough forms. Roll into a ball, then flatten into a disc before wrapping in clingfilm/plastic wrap. Chill for at least 30 minutes before using.

Preheat the oven to 200°C (400°F) Gas 6.

Cut the broccoli and cauliflower florets into chunks slightly larger than cherry tomatoes. Boil until al dente, then drain and set aside to cool.

Heat the oil in a frying pan/skillet and fry the onion until soft and golden. Set aside to cool slightly.

Remove the clingfilm/plastic wrap from the pastry and roll it out on a lightly floured surface, with a rolling pin, until it is slightly larger than the tart pan. Gently and loosely roll the pastry around the rolling pin and transfer it to the prepared tart pan. Line the pan with the pastry, pressing it into the fluted edges of the pan and neatly cutting off the excess pastry.

Tip the onion and any remaining oil from the pan into the pastry case and spread evenly. Top with the broccoli, cauliflower and cherry tomatoes. Sprinkle the cheeses evenly over the top and season with black pepper. Bake in the preheated oven for 25 minutes, or until golden brown. Serve warm or cold.

Ricotta and green herb torta

Italian olive oil pastry

500 g/4 cups plain/all-
purpose flour, plus
extra for rolling

1–2 teaspoons fine sea
salt flakes

4 tablespoons extra virgin
olive oil, plus extra to
drizzle

150 ml/⅔ cup warm water

Filling

500 g/1 lb. mixed greens

30 g/2 tablespoons
unsalted butter

½ onion, very finely
chopped

200 g/7 oz. ricotta, soft
goat's cheese or cream
cheese

140 g/2 cups grated
Parmesan

2 teaspoons plain/
all-purpose flour

2 tablespoons chopped
fresh marjoram

3 large eggs, beaten

salt and freshly ground
black pepper

*a deep 30-cm/12-in. tart
pan, lightly oiled*

SERVES 6–8

Torta usually means 'cake' in Italy, but in the Lunigiana and Liguria regions a torta is a filled savoury pie containing greens (or vegetables) and cheese, which can be served as an appetizer or a main course. They are normally eaten at room temperature to appreciate the delicate flavours. Balance the more assertive-flavoured greens with milder ones. Try a mix of beetroot tops/beet greens, spinach or Swiss chard or even spring greens mixed with rocket/arugula, mustard greens and some watercress.

To make the pastry, put the flour in a large mixing bowl and make a well in the middle with your fist. Add the salt and the olive oil, then pour in 150 ml/⅔ cup warm water, a little at a time (you may not need it all). Mix to form a soft dough, then use your hands to bring it together, kneading it gently into a ball for about 2 minutes – just long enough to become smooth to the touch. Seal the dough in a plastic bag and leave to rest for 1 hour at room temperature.

Preheat the oven to 190°C (375°F) Gas 5.

Wash the greens and remove any tough stems. While still wet, steam the greens using only the water that clings to their leaves. Squeeze them dry and chop coarsely.

Melt the butter in a small saucepan set over medium heat, add the onion and cook until soft and translucent. Stir in the chopped greens and cook for 2–3 minutes to heat through and coat with the butter. Remove the pan from the heat, leave to cool, then transfer the onion and greens to a large mixing bowl and beat in the ricotta, Parmesan, flour, marjoram, eggs, salt and plenty of pepper.

Once the pastry dough has rested, cut it into 2 pieces (one slightly larger than the other) and roll each piece out as thinly as you can on a lightly floured surface. Use the larger piece to line the pan, making sure that the pastry overhangs the edges.

Fill the lined pan with the cheese and greens mix, then cover with the remaining sheet of pastry. Press the edges together and trim off the excess dough. Crimp or turn the edges inwards in a rope fashion to seal the pie – it should look quite rustic! Make a couple of long slits in the top with a sharp knife. Drizzle a little olive oil on top of the crust and bake in the preheated oven for 40 minutes or until the crust is set and golden.

Serve warm or at room temperature.

Ricotta, sausage and potato pizza pie

In an ideal world this tastes best cooked in a wood–fired Sicilian pizza oven, but it is still hearty and delicious when baked in a more humdrum yet nice and hot domestic oven.

Sicilian pizza dough

7 g/¼ oz. fresh yeast, 1 teaspoon dried active baking yeast, or ½ teaspoon fast-action yeast

a pinch of sugar

150 ml/⅔ cup hand-hot water

250 g/2 cups fine semolina flour or durum wheat flour

½ teaspoon fine sea salt flakes

1 tablespoon olive oil, plus extra for brushing

1 tablespoon freshly squeezed lemon juice

Filling

2 tablespoons extra virgin olive oil

200 g/7 oz. potatoes, finely diced

2 onions, finely chopped

2 teaspoons dried oregano

250 g/9 oz. fresh Italian sausages, skinned

2 teaspoons tomato purée/paste

1 teaspoon fennel seeds

2 tablespoons chopped fresh sage

3 large eggs, beaten

125 g/4½ oz. ricotta

salt and freshly ground black pepper

a large lipless baking sheet

SERVES 6–8

In a medium bowl, cream the yeast with the sugar and whisk in the water. Leave for 10 minutes until frothy. For other yeasts, follow the manufacturer's instructions.

Sift the flour and salt into a mixing bowl and make a well in the centre. Pour in the yeast mixture, oil and lemon juice. Mix with a round-bladed knife, then your hands until the dough comes together. Add more water if necessary – the dough should be very soft. Tip out onto a lightly floured surface and knead briskly for at least 10 minutes until smooth, shiny and elastic. Try not to add any extra flour at this stage – it should be quite soft. If you feel that the dough is sticky, flour your hands and not the dough. When ready, shape into a neat ball, place in a clean, oiled bowl, cover with a damp kitchen cloth and leave to rise in a warm place until doubled in size – about 1½ hours.

Punch the air out of the dough, then transfer to a floured surface. Divide into two pieces (one piece slightly larger than the other) and shape both into a smooth ball. Place the balls well apart on a sheet of floured non-stick baking parchment, cover with clingfilm/plastic wrap and leave to rise for 60–90 minutes.

Place the baking sheet on the lower shelf of the oven and preheat it to 220°C (425°F) Gas 7 for at least 30 minutes.

Heat the oil in a frying pan/skillet and add the potato and onion. Cook for 5–10 minutes until the onions start to colour, and the potato is soft (add a spoonful of water if the vegetables look as if they are drying out). Stir in the oregano, season and transfer to a bowl to cool. Fry the sausage very briefly, breaking it up with the back of a fork, and add the tomato purée/paste, fennel seeds and sage. Season well, then let cool. In a separate bowl, beat the eggs into the ricotta.

Punch the air out of the the dough again. Roll out the smaller ball (the base) to a 25-cm/10-in. circle and the larger piece (the lid) to a 30-cm/12-in. disc, rolling the dough directly onto baking parchment. Spoon the potato and onion mixture onto the base and dot with the sausage. Spoon over the ricotta and egg mix and season well. Brush the edge with water and lay the lid on top, rolling the edges to seal. Brush with a little olive oil and make two or three holes in the top of the pie.

Working quickly, open the oven door and slide parchment and all onto the hot baking sheet. Bake for 10 minutes, then pull the parchment out from beneath the pie. Bake for a further 25–30 minutes until the crust is puffed up and golden. Remove from the oven and brush with a little olive oil. Leave to stand for 5 minutes before serving.

Goat's cheese, mushroom and rosemary pithivier

Golden puff pastry filled with goat's cheese, sliced mushrooms and walnuts, and marked in the sort of Catherine wheel pattern typical of Pithiviers: this would make any vegetarian feel special. Either make one large one for a crowd, or several smaller individual ones. It is good served with a generous spoonful of tomato and basil confit.

5 tablespoons extra virgin olive oil

2 garlic cloves, roughly chopped

1 tablespoon chopped fresh rosemary

300 g/10 oz. large dark open-cup mushrooms, thickly sliced

350 g/12 oz. leeks, trimmed and sliced

1 kg/2¼ lb. prepared puff pastry dough

50 g/⅓ cup walnuts, chopped (not too finely)

200 g/7 oz. goat's cheese, crumbled

1 small egg, plus 1 egg yolk, beaten to glaze

salt and freshly ground black pepper

tomato and basil confit, to serve

a 27-cm/11-in. dinner plate
a large lipless baking sheet

SERVES 6

Put 3 tablespoons of the olive oil and the garlic and rosemary into a spice grinder and blitz until smooth. Tip into a sauté pan/skillet and add the mushrooms. Stir to coat, add 2 tablespoons water, salt and pepper and cook over medium heat for about 5 minutes until soft and all the liquid has disappeared. Spread out on a tray and let cool.

Heat the remaining oil in the sauté pan/skillet and sauté the leeks for about 5 minutes until soft. Season and leave to cool.

On a lightly floured surface, roll out half of the pastry to a rough circle that is just bigger than the dinner plate. Using the plate as a guide, cut out a circle around the plate with a sharp knife. Slide the pastry circle onto a heavy baking sheet.

Spoon the cooled leeks onto the pastry circle in an even layer, leaving a 2.5-cm/1-in. bare rim of pastry all round. Mix the mushrooms gently with the walnuts and goat's cheese and spoon evenly over the leeks. Lightly flatten the top, keeping the pastry edges clean. Brush the pastry edge with the beaten egg.

Roll out the second quantity of pastry into a rough circle a good bit larger than the plate (it must be big enough to drape over the filling comfortably). Using a rolling pin, lift it up and lay over the filling, unrolling as you go. Gently mould it around the filling and press down around the edge to seal. Trim the edge to a width of 2.5 cm/1 in. Hold a knife horizontally and use the sharp edge to tap the edge of the pastry all the way around the dish. Scallop the edges and brush all over with the beaten egg. Chill the pastry in the refrigerator for at least 30 minutes.

Preheat the oven to its hottest setting.

Once chilled, use the tip of a small sharp knife or scalpel to lightly score a wheel pattern on the surface of the pastry, being careful not to cut through the pastry. (The pie can be kept chilled like this overnight, ready to cook the next day.)

Bake the pie in the preheated oven for 10 minutes, then reduce the temperature to 220°C (425°F) Gas 7 and cook for a further 20–25 minutes until crisp and golden brown (lay a sheet of kitchen foil on top if it is browning too quickly). Remove from the oven and rest for 5 minutes before serving with tomato and basil confit.

Greek spinach, feta and oregano filo pie

If you have ever enjoyed a summer holiday in Greece, this will take you right back there. This simple but delicious pie makes for tasty picnic fare – it can be easily transported in its baking dish. If you are not partial to salty feta, then ricotta will work well instead.

2 tablespoons olive oil

1 bunch of spring onions/ scallions, finely sliced

2 garlic cloves, crushed

450 g/1 lb. young spinach leaves, washed

4 large eggs, beaten

200 g/7 oz. Greek feta, crumbled

1 teaspoon freeze-dried oregano

a large pinch of freshly grated nutmeg

finely grated zest of 1 lemon

4 large filo/phyllo pastry sheets (about 225 g/ 8 oz.)

75 g/5 tablespoons butter, melted

salt and freshly ground black pepper

a 25 x 20-cm/10 x 8-in. baking pan

SERVES 6

Preheat the oven to 190°C (375°F) Gas 5.

Heat the oil in a large saucepan, add the spring onions/scallions and garlic and sauté for 2 minutes. Pile in the spinach, cover with a lid and cook for 3 minutes over a high heat or until the leaves are just wilted. Tip into a sieve/strainer and press out the excess moisture. Transfer to a large mixing bowl and stir in the eggs, feta, oregano, nutmeg, lemon zest, a little salt and plenty of pepper, mixing well.

Brush the inside of the baking pan with melted butter. Carefully brush the filo/phyllo pastry sheets all over with melted butter.

Lay the first sheet of pastry in the pan, pressing it into the base and up the sides. Place the second sheet on top at 90 degrees, making sure the pastry will overhang the pan. Repeat with the remaining 2 sheets of pastry.

Spoon the filling into the pastry-lined pan and level. Fold over the overlapping pastry, brushing with more butter as necessary. Brush the top with the remaining butter.

Bake in the preheated oven for 50–60 minutes until the pastry is golden brown and crisp. Remove from the oven and cover with a clean kitchen cloth for 5 minutes to lightly soften the pastry before you mark it. With a sharp knife, mark the pie into 6 squares and leave to cool. Serve warm or cold.

TIP: For a neater look to the top of the pie, use only 3½ sheets of the filo/ phyllo pastry to line the pan, saving a half sheet to lay over the top and neaten the look. Brush with butter before baking.

Hot Sandwiches and Pizza

There is nothing more comforting than grilled cheese, and there are endless options for using different varieties of cheese in the filling, from Kimchi and Monterey Jack to Lobster, Tarragon Mayonnaise and Beaufort. For a supper the whole family will enjoy, a home-made pizza is always a winner, with the oozing and bubbling cheese topping providing the perfect contrast to the crisp base.

Balsamic mushrooms and Fontina sandwich

Tangy balsamic mushrooms offer an earthy foil to the richness of the melted Fontina. Like most grilled cheese sandwiches, this one goes well with tomato soup, but also works nicely with a hearty cream of mushroom soup.

30 g/2 tablespoons unsalted butter, plus extra for buttering
1 tablespoon vegetable oil
125 g/1⅔ cups white mushrooms, thinly sliced
1 shallot, diced
½ teaspoon dried thyme
3 tablespoons balsamic vinegar
1 teaspoon red wine vinegar
150 g/2 cups grated Fontina, or use thin slices
4 slices granary/granary-style bread
salt and freshly ground black pepper

SERVES 2

In a non-stick frying pan/skillet, combine the butter, oil, mushrooms, shallot and thyme over medium–high heat and cook, stirring occasionally, until everything is soft and deep golden in colour. Season well, add the vinegars and simmer until the liquid almost evaporates. Taste and adjust the seasoning. Butter each of the bread slices on one side and set aside.

Without turning the heat on, place two slices of bread in a large, non-stick frying pan/skillet, butter-side down. If you can only fit one slice in your pan, you'll need to cook one sandwich at a time. Spoon over half of the mushrooms and sprinkle half of the grated cheese on top in an even layer. Cover each slice with another bread slice, butter-side up.

Turn the heat to medium and cook the first side for 3–5 minutes until it turns a deep golden colour, pressing gently with a spatula. Carefully turn with the spatula and cook on the second side for 2–3 minutes, or until deep golden brown all over.

Remove from the frying pan/skillet, transfer to a plate and cut the sandwiches in half. Let cool for a few minutes before serving alongside a bowl of hot mushroom soup.

Kimchi and Monterey Jack sandwich

Melted cheese really benefits from something sour or tangy to act as a foil for the richness. Here, kimchi, a spiced Korean condiment of fermented pickled cabbage, does just that to perfection. The combination may sound strange at first, but it's fantastic. There's a good reason why kimchi is taking off around the world!

60 g/½ cup kimchi
150 g/1¾ cups grated
   mild cheese, such as
   Monterey Jack or mild
   Cheddar
4 slices white bread,
   crusts removed
unsalted butter, softened

SERVES 2

Butter each of the bread slices on one side and set aside.

Pat the kimchi dry with paper towels to remove excess moisture and chop.

Without turning the heat on, put two slices of bread in a large, heavy-based non-stick frying pan/skillet, butter-side down. If two slices won't fit, cook them in batches. Top with half the kimchi and sprinkle over half the grated cheese in an even layer. Cover with another bread slice, butter-side up.

Turn the heat to medium and cook the first side for 3–5 minutes until it turns a deep golden colour, pressing gently with a spatula. Carefully turn with the spatula and cook on the second side for 2–3 minutes, or until deep golden brown all over. Remove from the frying pan/skillet, transfer to a plate and cut in half. Let cool for a few minutes before serving. Repeat for the remaining sandwich if necessary.

NOTE: Vegetarians should be aware that kimchi often contains fish as part of the seasoning.

Blue cheese, Serrano ham and walnut pesto sandwich

1 large chicory/endive, halved and thinly sliced lengthwise
15 g/1 tablespoon butter
1 tablespoon vegetable oil
125 ml/½ cup dry white wine
4 slices white bread
unsalted butter, softened
90 g/3 oz. soft blue cheese, at room temperature
2 thin slices Gouda or Fontina
4–6 slices Serrano ham

Pesto
100 g/1 cup walnut pieces
80 g/1 cup grated Parmesan
a small bunch of flat-leaf parsley, leaves stripped
1 garlic clove
about 150 ml/⅔ cup rapeseed oil
a drizzle of runny honey
freshly squeezed juice of ½ lemon, or more to taste
salt and freshly ground black pepper

SERVES 2

Salty, bitter, sweet and nutty all collide in this decadent, Iberian-inspired sandwich. It is unusual as well as elegant so serve as a dinner party appetizer with a glass of chilled Spanish white, or try it for an out of the ordinary midweek supper.

For the walnut pesto, combine all the ingredients in a food processor and process until it forms a spreadable paste. Taste and add more salt, pepper and lemon juice as required. Set aside.

Combine the chicory/endive slices, butter and oil in a non-stick frying pan/skillet and cook over medium heat until soft and beginning to brown. Add the wine, boil for 1 minute, then season, lower the heat, cover and simmer for 5 minutes. Remove the lid and continue cooking gently until the liquid evaporates. Then, coarsely chop the chicory/endive and set aside.

Spread softened butter on each of the bread slices on one side. Spread two of the slices (non-buttered sides) with the blue cheese and spread the remaining two slices of bread (non-buttered sides) with pesto.

This is easiest if assembled in a large, heavy-based non-stick frying pan/skillet. Put the pesto-covered slices of bread in the pan, butter-side down. Top each with one slice of cheese, half of the chicory/endive and half of the ham. Finally, top with the blue cheese bread slices, butter-side up.

Turn the heat to medium and cook the first side for 3–5 minutes until deep golden, pressing gently with a spatula. Carefully turn with a large spatula and cook on the other side, for 2–3 minutes more or until deep golden brown all over.

Remove from the pan and transfer to a plate. Let cool for a few minutes before serving. Repeat for the remaining sandwich if necessary.

NOTE: Leftover pesto can be kept in the refrigerator in a sealed container.

Chorizo, Manchego and mini bell pepper sandwich

This decidedly Spanish-inspired treat features a magical combination of spicy, smoky chorizo, sweet mini (bell) peppers and creamy Manchego. If you want a little extra ooziness, replace some of the Manchego with mozzarella. If you're a spice fan, why not substitute the sweet (bell) peppers for Padrón peppers for an extra kick.

1–2 tablespoons extra virgin olive oil
100 g/3½ oz. mini (bell) peppers or Padrón peppers
unsalted butter, softened
4 slices sourdough or other artisan bread
100 g/3½ oz. chorizo, thinly sliced
250 g/3 cups grated Manchego
salt

SERVES 2

Heat the oil in a small frying pan/skillet and add the peppers. Cook over medium heat until charred all over; 5–10 minutes. Season lightly with salt and set aside.

Butter the bread slices on one side and arrange buttered-side down on a clean work surface or chopping board.

Divide the chorizo in half and arrange on two slices of bread. Next, divide the cheese in half and sprinkle two-thirds of each on top. Top with three or four peppers, then the remaining cheese. Enclose with the remaining bread, buttered-side up.

Place the two sandwiches in a large, heavy-based non-stick frying pan/skillet. Depending on the size of your pan, you may need to cook one sandwich at a time.

Turn the heat to medium and cook for 3–4 minutes on the first side. Carefully turn with a large spatula and cook on the second side, for 2–3 minutes more, pressing down gently on this side until golden brown all over.

Remove from the pan and transfer to a plate. Leave to cool for a few minutes before serving.

Tartiflette sandwich

A fried potato sandwich, layered with wine-infused melting onions and Reblochon cheese – food does not get much better. To counteract all the carbs, serve with a salad of sliced lettuce drizzled with a tangy, mustardy vinaigrette. Maybe follow with a brisk walk, or a nap, as mood dictates!

425 g/15 oz. waxy potatoes, peeled and thinly sliced

1 tablespoon vegetable oil

1 medium onion, thinly sliced

a knob/pat of butter

1–2 slices pancetta or bacon, finely chopped

½ teaspoon dried thyme

4 tablespoons dry white wine

30 g/2 tablespoons unsalted butter, melted

1 medium baguette, cut in two lengthways and widthways

160 g/5½ oz. Reblochon, chilled and thinly sliced

salt and freshly ground black pepper

a small baking dish, generously greased with butter

SERVES 2

Preheat the oven to 190°C (375°F) Gas 5.

Arrange the potato slices in the prepared dish, drizzle over the oil and sprinkle with salt. Roast for 20–30 minutes, turning once, until brown around the edges and tender.

Meanwhile, put the onion slices in a small frying pan/skillet with the knob/pat of butter and cook over medium heat, stirring occasionally, until golden and soft. Add the pancetta and thyme and cook for a few minutes more. Add the wine and cook until evaporated. Season lightly and set aside.

Brush the outsides of the bread with the melted butter. Arrange butter-side down on a clean work surface or chopping board. Arrange half the cheese, potatoes and onions over the two bottom halves. Finally, place the top halves of baguette on top, butter-side up.

Place the sandwiches in a large, heavy-based non-stick frying pan/skillet. Depending on the size of your pan, you may need to cook one sandwich at a time.

Turn the heat to medium and cook the first side for 3–4 minutes until deep golden, pressing gently with a spatula. Carefully turn with a large spatula and cook on the other side for 2–3 minutes more or until deep golden brown all over.

Remove from the pan and allow to cool for a few minutes before serving. Repeat for the remaining sandwich if necessary.

Lobster tail, tarragon mayonnaise and Beaufort sandwich

For many people, pairing seafood with cheese should never be done. However, if any cheese were able to partner lobster, 'le roi' of the seafood set, it would have to be Beaufort, one of the best cheeses in the world. Add tarragon-flecked mayonnaise and, suddenly, the impossible seems possible. Give it a try.

2–3 tablespoons
   mayonnaise
a small handful of
   tarragon leaves,
   freshly chopped
1 teaspoon freshly
   squeezed lemon juice
4 large slices brioche
about 250 g/9 oz. lobster
   meat, cooked
250 g/3 cups grated
   Beaufort
unsalted butter, softened
coarse, freshly ground
   black pepper

SERVES 2

In a small bowl, combine the mayonnaise, tarragon, lemon juice and a generous pinch of black pepper. Stir well and set aside.

Butter the bread slices on one side and arrange buttered-side down on a clean work surface or a chopping board. Spread two of the non-buttered sides generously with the tarragon mayonnaise.

Assemble just before cooking, in a large, heavy-based non-stick frying pan/skillet. Depending on the size of your pan, you may need to cook one sandwich at a time. If it is large enough, place the two bread slices not spread with tarragon mayonnaise in the pan, buttered-side down. Top each of these slices with half of the cheese, taking care not to let too much fall into the pan. Top this with half the lobster, arranging in an even layer over all. Finally, top with the mayonnaise-coated slices of bread, buttered-side up.

Turn the heat to medium and cook the first side for 3–4 minutes until deep golden, pressing gently with a large spatula. Carefully turn with the spatula and cook on the other side for 2–3 minutes more or until deep golden brown all over.

Remove from the pan and let cool for a few minutes before serving. Repeat for the remaining sandwich if necessary.

Burger Scamorza

Scamorza is an Italian smoked cheese, similar to mozzarella in that it has the same beautiful melting quality, but with a little more punch. The burger for this sandwich needs to be thin-ish for ease of cooking and eating. Add some crispy cooked bacon, if you like. Serve the burgers with fries, naturally.

250 g/9 oz. minced/
    ground beef
1 small onion, grated
½ teaspoon garlic powder
½ teaspoon salt
a dash of Worcestershire
    sauce (optional)
2 white burger buns
300 g/10½ oz. scamorza
    or mozzarella, sliced
vegetable oil
freshly ground black
    pepper
tomato ketchup, to serve
gherkin/pickle spears,
    to serve
fries, to serve

SERVES 2

In a mixing bowl, combine the minced/ground beef, onion, garlic powder, salt, Worcestershire sauce, if using, and some black pepper. Mix well. Shape into two thin patties.

Slice the burger buns in half widthways. Brush the bun halves lightly on the outside with vegetable oil.

Heat up some vegetable oil in a large, heavy-based non-stick frying pan/skillet over medium heat. When the pan is hot, cook the burgers for 3–5 minutes on each side, depending on how well-done you like your meat. Transfer the cooked burgers to a plate and set aside.

Clean the frying pan/skillet. If space allows, place two bun halves, oil-side down in the pan/skillet (without turning the heat on), but you may have to cook them one at a time if they won't fit in the pan. Top each slice with one-quarter of the scamorza or mozzarella slices, then carefully place the burger on top. Follow this with another quarter of the cheese, so that the meat is nicely surrounded by cheese. Finally, cover with the tops of the buns, oil-side up.

Turn the heat to medium and cook the first side for 3–5 minutes until deep golden, pressing gently with a spatula. Carefully turn with a large spatula and cook on the other side, for 2–3 minutes more or until deep golden brown all over.

Let cool for a few minutes before serving with fries, ketchup and gherkin/pickle spears. Repeat for the remaining sandwich if necessary.

Tricolore French toast

This savoury French toast recipe is delicious filled with the classic combination of mozzarella, basil and sundried tomatoes. Serve with a green salad on the side, or even wrapped up for a picnic lunch.

4 thick slices bread

150–200 g/1–1½ cups
mozzarella, thinly sliced

12 sundried tomatoes

a handful of basil leaves,
freshly chopped

2 eggs

60 ml/¼ cup milk

15–30 g/1–2 tablespoons
butter, for frying

salt and freshly ground
black pepper

a large frying pan/skillet
or griddle

SERVES 4

Using a sharp knife, cut a pocket in the top of each slice of bread to create a large cavity. Take care not to cut all the way through as it is this cavity which will hold your filling. Stuff each slice with the mozzarella, tomatoes and a little of the basil. Press the opening down to close the pocket.

Whisk together the egg and milk in a large mixing bowl and season with salt and pepper, then whisk in the remaining basil. Melt the butter in a large frying pan/skillet set over medium heat until the butter begins to foam. Soak each sandwich in the beaten egg mixture on one side for a few seconds, then turn over and soak the other side. The slices should be fully coated in egg, but not too soggy – it is best to soak one slice at a time. Put each sandwich straight in the pan before soaking and cooking the next toast.

Cook for 2–3 minutes on each side until the egg is cooked and the slices are lightly golden brown and the cheese has melted. Keep the toasts warm while you cook the remaining sandwiches.

Serve immediately.

Chipotle, black bean and feta quesadilla with Pico de Gallo

3 tablespoons vegetable
   oil
1 onion, diced
3 garlic cloves, crushed/
   minced
1 teaspoon dried oregano
1 teaspoon ground cumin
a pinch of ground
   cinnamon
2 chipotle chillies/chiles
   in adobo sauce, finely
   chopped
200 g/1 cup passata/
   strained tomatoes
2 x 400-g/14-oz. cans
   black beans, drained
8 large flour tortillas
200 g/2 cups feta cheese
   or queso fresco,
   crumbled
salt
sour cream, to serve

Pico de Gallo
6–8 ripe tomatoes
1 large red onion, finely
   chopped
1 fresh green chilli/chile,
   or more to taste, finely
   chopped
1 bunch fresh coriander/
   cilantro
½ teaspoon salt
freshly squeezed juice
   of 1 lime
freshly squeezed lemon
   juice, optional

SERVES 4–6

The smoky taste of chipotle is irresistible mixed with the warmth of the cinnamon and the salty tang of the cheese. For an authentic Mexican taste, replace the feta with queso fresco. Pico de Gallo is so tasty, it can be a filling on its own.

Preheat the oven to 120°C (250°F) Gas ½.

To make Pico de Gallo, put the tomatoes, onion, chilli/chile and coriander/cilantro in a small bowl. Add the salt and lime juice and toss well. Let stand for at least 1 hour or cover and refrigerate overnight. Taste and adjust the seasoning, adding more chilli/chile or a squeeze of lemon juice if desired. Chill until needed, then serve at room temperature.

Heat 2 tablespoons of the oil in a saucepan set over medium–high heat. Add the onion and cook for 5–8 minutes, stirring occasionally, until golden. Add the garlic, oregano, cumin and cinnamon and cook for 1–2 minutes, stirring often. Add the chopped chillies/chiles and cook for 1 minute more, stirring often. Stir in the passata/strained tomatoes, beans, a pinch of salt and 60 ml/¼ cup water and cover. Simmer for 15 minutes then taste and adjust the seasoning.

To assemble the quesadillas, spread one-quarter of the bean mixture on four of the tortillas. Sprinkle each with one-quarter of the crumbled cheese and top with another tortilla.

Heat the remaining oil in a non-stick frying pan/skillet set over medium heat. When hot, add a quesadilla, lower the heat and cook for 2–3 minutes until golden on one side and the cheese begins to melt. Turn over and cook the other side for 2–3 minutes. Transfer to a heatproof plate and keep warm in the preheated oven while you cook the rest.

To serve, top each quesadilla with sour cream and Pico de Gallo. Cut into wedges and serve immediately.

Irresistible Italian four-cheese pizza

Pizza dough

150 g/1 cup strong white bread flour

125 g/scant 1 cup Italian '00' flour

1 teaspoon salt

1 teaspoon fast-action dried yeast

½ teaspoon sugar

2 tablespoons olive oil, plus extra to drizzle

about 175 ml/¾ cup hand-hot water

semolina or cornmeal/ polenta, to dust the baking sheets

Topping

400 ml/1¾ cups passata/ strained tomatoes

150 g/5½ oz. pecorino Toscano (rind removed), sliced

150 g/5½ oz. Taleggio (rind removed) or buffalo mozzarella, sliced

90 g/3 oz. Gorgonzola piccante, crumbled

30 g/1 oz. Parmesan, grated

a small handful of oregano or basil leaves

freshly ground black pepper

2 large baking sheets, lightly oiled

MAKES 2 PIZZAS

Pizza 'quattro formaggi' sometimes has a reputation for being bland and indigestible, but just try making it with top-quality Italian cheeses and you will taste the difference.

To make the pizza dough, sift the two flours into a bowl along with the salt, yeast and sugar. Mix together, then form a hollow in the centre. Add the olive oil and half the hand-hot water and stir to incorporate the flour. Gradually add as much of the remaining water as you need to pull the dough together. (It should take most of it – you need a wettish dough.) Turn the dough out onto a board and knead for 10 minutes until smooth and elastic, adding a little extra flour to prevent the dough sticking if necessary. Put the dough into a lightly oiled bowl, cover with clingfilm/plastic wrap and leave in a warm place until doubled in size; about 1–1¼ hours.

Preheat the oven to 240°C (475°F) Gas 9 and sprinkle the prepared baking sheets with semolina.

Tip the dough out of the bowl and press down on it to knock out the air. Divide it in half. Pull and shape one piece of dough into a large circle, then place it on a prepared baking sheet and push it out towards the edges of the sheet. (It doesn't have to be a perfect circle!) Spread half the passata/strained tomatoes over the top, then arrange half the cheeses over the top. Season with pepper. Repeat with the other piece of dough and the remaining cheese.

Drizzle a little olive oil over the top of each pizza and bake in the preheated oven for 8–10 minutes, or until the dough has puffed up and the cheese is brown and bubbling. Garnish the pizzas with oregano leaves and drizzle over a little more oil.

Pizza with artichokes and mozzarella

Artichokes preserved in oil for antipasti are perfect for pizza–making as the delicious oil they are soaked in means they won't dry out during cooking. You can also make this with smoked mozzarella and it is equally delicious.

1 quantity Pizza Dough (see page 104)

200 g/7 oz. buffalo mozzarella

200 g/7 oz. artichokes preserved in oil (or grilled artichokes from a deli)

2–3 garlic cloves, finely chopped

4 tablespoons extra virgin olive oil, plus extra to drizzle

16 black olives

4 tablespoons freshly chopped flat leaf parsley (optional)

salt and freshly ground black pepper

semolina or cornmeal/ polenta, to dust the baking sheets

2 large baking sheets, lightly oiled

MAKES 4 MINI PIZZAS

Preheat the oven to 240°C (475°F) Gas 9 and sprinkle the prepared baking sheets with semolina.

Lightly squeeze any excess moisture out of the mozzarella, then slice it and leave the slices on paper towels for 5 minutes to absorb any remaining moisture. Cut the artichokes into quarters and toss them with the garlic and olive oil.

Tip the dough out of the bowl and press down on it to knock out the air. Divide it in quarters. Pull and shape one piece of dough into a small circle, then place it on a prepared baking sheet and push it out towards the edges of the sheet. Repeat with the other pieces of dough, putting two bases on each baking sheet.

Arrange the mozzarella evenly over the pizza bases, leaving a 1-cm/½-in. rim around the edge. Scatter the artichoke and olives over the mozzarella, then season and drizzle with olive oil.

Bake in the preheated oven for 8–10 minutes, or until the crust is golden and the cheese melted and bubbling. Remove from the oven and sprinkle the parsley, if using, and freshly ground pepper over the top. Eat immediately.

Pear, pecorino and Taleggio pizza with honey and sage

This is a sort of new-wave pizza, and very popular in Italian city pizzerias. Soft, buttery Taleggio, made in the valleys and mountains of Lombardy and the Valtellina, melts and runs very quickly, so make sure it's not near the edge of the pizza. Ripe, juicy pear is the perfect foil for this cheese, and don't leave out the sage – it's integral to the flavour.

1 quantity Pizza Dough (see page 104)

4 tablespoons extra virgin olive oil, plus extra to drizzle

250 g/8 oz. Taleggio (rind removed), cubed

2 very ripe pears, cored and thinly sliced

a handful of small sage leaves

100 g/3½ oz. freshly grated pecorino

2 tablespoons runny honey (acacia or orange blossom, if possible)

salt and freshly ground black pepper

semolina or cornmeal/polenta, to dust the baking sheets

2 large baking sheets, lightly oiled

MAKES 2 PIZZAS

Preheat the oven to 240°C (475°F) Gas 9 and sprinkle the prepared baking sheets with semolina.

Tip the dough out of the bowl and press down on it to knock out the air. Divide it in half. Pull and shape one piece of dough into a large circle, then place it on a prepared baking sheet and push it out towards the edges of the sheet. (It doesn't have to be a perfect circle!) Repeat with the second piece of dough.

Rub the pizza bases with the olive oil and scatter over the Taleggio. Arrange the pears over this, then the sage and pecorino. Drizzle with the honey, then season and drizzle with a little more olive oil.

Bake in the preheated oven for 8–10 minutes, or until the crust is golden and the cheese melted and bubbling. Sprinkle with freshly ground black pepper and eat immediately.

Potato pizza with Fontina

In general, Italians like to stick to the classics when it comes to pizza, but as you can see below, pizza toppings are limitless. This pizza is made in a rectangular baking pan.

Pizza dough

15 g/½ oz. fresh yeast, 1 tablespoon dried active baking yeast, or 1 sachet easy-blend yeast

a pinch of sugar

250 ml/1 cup warm water

350 g/2⅓ cups plain/ all-purpose white flour, plus extra for dusting

1 tablespoon olive oil

a pinch of salt

Topping

1 medium potato, peeled and sliced extremely thinly

150 g/5½ oz. Fontina, Taleggio or mozzarella

1 large radicchio, cut into about 8 wedges, brushed with olive oil and grilled/broiled for 5 minutes

1 tablespoon freshly chopped thyme

salt and freshly ground black pepper

extra olive oil, for trickling

a baking pan, about 23 x 33 cm/9 x 13 in.

SERVES 2–4

To make the dough, put the fresh yeast and sugar in a medium bowl and beat until creamy. Whisk in the warm water and leave for 10 minutes until frothy. For other yeasts, use according to the package instructions.

Sift the flour into a large bowl and make a hollow in the centre. Pour in the yeast mixture, olive oil and a good pinch of salt. Mix with a round-bladed knife, then your hands, until the dough comes together. Transfer to a floured surface, wash and dry your hands and knead for 10 minutes until smooth and elastic. The dough should be quite soft, but if too soft to handle, add more flour, 1 tablespoon at a time. Put the dough in a clean, oiled bowl, cover with a damp kitchen cloth or clingfilm/plastic wrap and let rise until doubled in size; about 1 hour.

Preheated oven to 220°C (425°F) Gas 7.

When risen, punch down the dough with your fists, then roll out or pat into a rectangle that will fit in the baking pan, pushing it up the sides a little. Cover the top with a thin layer of sliced potato, then half the cheese, the wedges of radicchio, then the remaining cheese. Season with salt and pepper, and sprinkle with thyme.

Trickle oil over the top and let rise in a warm place for 10 minutes. Bake in the preheated oven for 15–20 minutes or until golden and bubbling.

Frittatas, Omelettes and Pancakes

Eggs are the ultimate healthy fast food, and in this chapter you will find plenty of quick, easy and tasty meals for brunches, lunches and light suppers. Frittatas, omelettes and pancakes will go with almost any type of cheese, whether a soft ricotta or a firm Spanish Manchego. Quickly sizzled in a frying pan/skillet or cooked under a hot grill/broiler, there is ample opportunity for melting golden gooeyness.

Asparagus, sweetcorn and goat's cheese frittata

The frittata is a brilliant stand-by for a no-fuss, fast supper. Crunchy asparagus and sweetcorn work nicely here combined with farm-fresh eggs, creamy goat's cheese and fresh, tangy dill. It's an Italian-style omelette, often cooked slowly and still slightly moist when served. If you prefer your eggs a bit firmer, leave under the hot grill/broiler for a little longer.

2 bunches of thin asparagus spears
2 fresh corn-on-the-cobs
50 g/3½ tablespoons butter
4 spring onions/scallions, finely chopped
2 tablespoons freshly chopped dill
8 eggs, beaten
200 g/1½ cups goat's cheese, broken into pieces
sea salt flakes and freshly ground black pepper

SERVES 4

Trim, or snap off, the woody ends from the asparagus and cut the spears into 2–3-cm/¾–1¼-in. pieces. Shuck the corn kernels from the cobs.

Heat half of the butter in a large non-stick frying pan/skillet set over medium heat. Add the asparagus, sweetcorn and spring onions/scallions and fry for 2–3 minutes, stirring often. Transfer the vegetables to a large bowl and add the dill, reserving a little to use as garnish. Wipe the pan clean. Add the beaten eggs to the vegetables, gently stirring to combine, and season well with salt and pepper.

Preheat the grill/broiler to high. Put the remaining butter in the frying pan/skillet and set over high heat. Swirl the pan around as the butter melts so that it coats the bottom and just starts to sizzle. Pour the frittata mixture into the pan and reduce the heat to medium. Arrange the pieces of goat's cheese over the top of the frittata and gently push them into the mixture. Cook for about 8 minutes, until the sides of the frittata start to puff up (reduce the heat if the bottom appears to be cooking too quickly).

Keep the fritatta in the frying pan/skillet and place it under the preheated grill/broiler. Cook for 1 minute only just to set the top. Let cool a little in the pan, sprinkle with the reserved dill and serve immediately.

Goat's cheese omelette with wild garlic/ramps and chervil

If you haven't had goat's cheese in an omelette before, do try it – it has a real affinity with eggs. Wild garlic/ramps adds pleasant texture as well as flavour, and you can buy these at farmers' markets or greengrocers.

a small handful of fresh
    chervil or parsley
2 large or 3 medium eggs
2 wild garlic/ramps
    leaves, finely shredded,
    or some finely snipped
    fresh chives
15 g/1 tablespoon butter
40 g/¼ cup goat's cheese,
    crumbled
sea salt flakes and freshly
    ground black pepper

SERVES 1

Pick over the chervil, cutting away the tougher stems, and chop finely. Beat the eggs in a bowl with a splash of water (about 1 tablespoon), add the chopped chervil and wild garlic/ramps leaves and beat again. Season with salt and pepper.

Heat a medium-sized frying pan/skillet or omelette pan until hot, add the butter, swirl it around and pour in the beaten eggs and herbs, swirling them around the pan. Lift the edge of the omelette as it begins to cook, letting the liquid egg run from the centre to the edge. Scatter over the goat's cheese and leave for a minute to allow the omelette to brown. Add more pepper if you like.

Fold one side of the omelette over and tip it onto a plate. You could serve this with some lightly dressed mixed salad leaves.

Red bell pepper and Manchego tortilla

The addition of cheese to a tortilla makes it substantial enough for a main course, as well as a stylish tapas dish. You may feel it's time-consuming to fry the vegetables separately but you'll find that it enormously improves the flavour and texture of the finished dish.

6 tablespoons extra virgin olive oil, plus extra to fry

1 large onion, very thinly sliced

1 large, red (bell) pepper, quartered, deseeded and finely sliced

350 g/2½ cups salad potatoes, e.g. Charlotte, very thinly sliced

8 eggs

75 g/½ cup Manchego, thinly sliced

sea salt flakes and freshly ground black pepper

SERVES 4–6

Heat 4 tablespoons of the oil in a large, deep lidded frying pan/skillet or wok, then fry the onion and (bell) pepper over medium heat until soft. Remove from the pan with a slotted spoon, leaving behind the oil.

Add the remaining oil to the frying pan/skillet, heat for 1 minute, then tip in the potatoes and stir with a spatula to ensure the slices are separate and well coated in oil. Fry, stirring, for about 5–6 minutes until they start to brown, then reduce the heat, cover with the lid and cook for another 10–15 minutes until the potatoes are tender, turning them every so often so that they don't catch.

Tip the onion and (bell) pepper back into the pan, mix with the potatoes and continue to fry (uncovered) for another 5 minutes. Season generously with salt and pepper and set aside for 10 minutes or so to cool.

Break the eggs into a large bowl and beat lightly. Tip the contents of the pan and the Manchego into the beaten eggs and mix gently. Heat your pan again until moderately hot, add a little oil, wipe off the excess with paper towels, then pour in the egg mixture. Lift the edge of the tortilla as it begins to cook, letting the liquid egg run from the centre to the edge. Cook until most of the egg has set, then reduce the heat a little and cook for about 3–4 minutes. Meanwhile, preheat the grill/broiler to medium.

Slip the frying pan/skillet under the grill/broiler about 12 cm/4¾ in. from the heat and leave until the top of the tortilla has puffed up and lightly browned and the egg in the middle has set (about 4 minutes). Remove from under the grill/broiler and leave to cool for about 30 minutes in the pan, then loosen it around the edge. Place a plate over the pan and flip the tortilla over so that it lands bottom-side upwards. Cut into wedges and serve at room temperature.

Taleggio and potato tortilla with tapenade

This is simple tapas-style food for sharing at its best. The tortilla may not look that substantial, but thanks to the creamy Taleggio cheese, it packs a super-rich taste punch and is more than enough for four to enjoy as an appetizer or snack. Keep your eyes peeled for nice little new potatoes when you are out shopping. Sometimes you will only be able to find waxies that are the size of a golf ball, but at other times you'll see deliciously nutty little potatoes (the size of a shelled walnut) like the ones used here. The red (bell) pepper tapenade is a very versatile recipe to have in your repertoire. It can be tossed through cooked pasta, spooned over grilled fish or chicken and stirred into soup.

10–12 small, waxy new potatoes, thickly sliced
1 small red onion, roughly chopped
1 tablespoon olive oil
250 ml/1 cup vegetable stock
2 tablespoons freshly chopped flat leaf parsley
100 g/1 cup Taleggio, chopped or torn into large chunks
2 eggs, lightly beaten

Tapenade
1 large red (bell) pepper
1 garlic clove, chopped
50 g/⅓ cup pine nuts/ kernels, toasted
2 tablespoons olive oil
50 g/generous ½ cup Parmesan, finely grated

SERVES 4

To make the tapenade, preheat the oven to 220°C (425°F) Gas 7. Put a baking sheet in the oven for a few minutes to heat. Put the red (bell) pepper on the warmed baking sheet and cook it in the preheated oven for about 15 minutes, turning often until the skin is starting to blacken and puff up. Transfer it to a clean plastic bag and let cool. When the (bell) pepper is cool enough to handle, peel off the skin, roughly tear or chop the flesh and put it in a food processor. Add the garlic, pine nuts/kernels and oil and process until smooth. Spoon into a bowl, add the Parmesan and stir well to combine.

Put the potatoes, onion and oil in a frying pan/skillet set over high heat and cook for 1 minute. Add the stock and cook for about 10 minutes, until the stock has evaporated and the vegetables start to sizzle in the pan. Stir through the parsley and put the pieces of cheese among the potatoes.

Pour the eggs into the frying pan/skillet and cook for 2–3 minutes until they start to puff up around the edges. Give the pan a couple of firm shakes – this will make it easier to get the cooked tortilla out of the pan. Meanwhile, preheat the grill/broiler to high.

Put the frying pan/skillet under the hot grill/broiler and cook the tortilla for 1–2 minutes, until the top is golden but still wobbly in the centre. Use a spatula to smear some of the tapenade onto the base of a serving plate and carefully slide the tortilla onto the plate. Cut into 4 slices and eat with extra tapenade on the side.

Courgette/zucchini and feta griddle cakes

These little pancakes are quick and easy to prepare and make a great accompaniment to soups as an alternative to bread. The feta cheese melts when cooked, giving them a lovely soft texture. You can make these with raw courgette/zucchini, but if you prefer you can fry them until soft in a little olive oil before adding to the pancake batter. Make sure that you drain the courgette/zucchini of its cooking juices and cool first.

150 g/heaped 1 cup self-raising/rising flour, sifted

2 eggs, separated

250 ml/1 cup milk

70 g/4 tablespoons plus 1 teaspoon butter, melted and cooled, plus extra for frying

1 teaspoon baking powder

1 large grated courgette/zucchini (approx. 200 g/ 2½ cups)

200 g/1½ cups feta, crumbled

1 tablespoon freshly chopped mint

sea salt flakes and freshly ground black pepper, to taste

MAKES 10

To make the pancake batter, put the flour, egg yolks, milk, melted butter and baking powder in a large mixing bowl and whisk together. Season well with salt and pepper and mix again until you have a smooth batter.

In a separate bowl, whisk the egg whites to stiff peaks. Gently fold the whisked egg whites into the batter mixture using a spatula. Cover and put in the refrigerator to rest for 30 minutes.

When you are ready to serve, remove the batter mixture from the refrigerator and stir gently. Add the grated courgette/zucchini to the batter with the feta and mint.

Put a little butter in a large frying pan/skillet set over medium heat. Allow the butter to melt and coat the base of the pan, then ladle small amounts of the rested batter into the pan, leaving a little space between each. Cook until the underside of each pancake is golden brown and a few bubbles start to appear on the top – this will take about 2–3 minutes. Turn the pancake over using a spatula and cook on the other side until golden brown. It is important that they cook all the way through to ensure that the middle of your pancakes are not soggy.

Serve immediately.

Squash and goat's cheese pancakes

1 butternut squash, peeled and seeds removed (670 g/2½ lb.), diced

2 tablespoons olive oil

1 teaspoon black onion seeds

a pinch of spiced (or regular) sea salt flakes

4–5 curry leaves, crushed

1–2 garlic cloves, skins on

200 g/1⅔ cups self-raising/rising flour, sifted

2 teaspoons baking powder

1 egg

300 ml/1¼ cups milk

60 g/3 tablespoons melted butter, plus extra for greasing

125 g/1 cup soft goat's cheese

sour cream or crème fraîche, to serve

a bunch of Greek basil leaves, to garnish

pumpkin seed oil, to drizzle

sea salt flakes and freshly ground black pepper, to taste

an ovenproof roasting pan, greased

SERVES 4

Perfect for lunch, these pancakes are topped with sour cream or crème fraîche and drizzled with delicious pumpkin seed oil. A mild, creamy goat's cheese gives a really nice contrast to the spiced squash.

Preheat the oven to 180°C (350°F) Gas 4.

Put the diced butternut squash in the prepared roasting pan. Drizzle with the olive oil and sprinkle over the onion seeds, salt and curry leaves. Stir so that the squash is well coated in the oil and spices, then add the garlic cloves to the pan. Roast in the preheated oven for 35–45 minutes until the squash is soft and starts to caramelize at the edges. Leave to cool completely.

To make the pancake batter, put the flour, baking powder, egg and milk in a large mixing bowl and whisk together. Season with salt and pepper. Add the melted butter and whisk again. The batter should have a smooth, dropping consistency. Add about two thirds of the butternut squash to the batter and set aside.

Remove the skins from the garlic cloves and mash to a paste using a fork. Whisk into the batter then crumble in the goat's cheese. Mix together gently. Cover and put in the refrigerator to rest for 30 minutes.

Put a little butter in a large frying pan/skillet set over a medium heat. Allow the butter to melt and coat the base of the pan, then ladle spoonfuls of the rested batter into the pan, leaving a little space between each. Cook until the underside of each pancake is golden brown and a few bubbles start to appear on the top – this will take about 2–3 minutes.

Turn the pancake over using a spatula and cook on the other side until golden brown.

Serve the pancakes, topped with a spoonful of sour cream, a few sprigs of basil and the reserved butternut squash. Drizzle with pumpkin seed oil and sprinkle with freshly ground black pepper.

Gluten-free spinach and ricotta crêpes

These delicate stuffed cheesy crêpes are such a treat, especially considering that they are fairly healthy. The batter is much thinner than traditional crêpe batter and the spinach makes them bright green in colour. Filled with ricotta, lemon and Parmesan – they are truly delicious.

80 g/⅔ cup buckwheat flour, sifted
200 ml/1 cup water
2 eggs
1–2 tablespoons butter, for greasing
sea salt flakes and freshly ground black pepper, to taste

Filling
400 g/8 cups spinach, washed and drained
250 g/1 cup ricotta
a pinch of freshly grated nutmeg
freshly squeezed juice of 1 unwaxed lemon plus 1 teaspoon of the grated zest
60 g/scant 1 cup Parmesan, plus extra to serve

a crêpe swizzle stick (optional)

SERVES 6

Begin by preparing the filling. Bring a large saucepan or pot of water to the boil over high heat and season with salt. Add the spinach to the pan and cook in the water for a few minutes until it is just wilted but still vibrant green. Drain and immediately plunge the spinach into cold water. Once cool, put the spinach in a clean kitchen cloth, fold up tightly and squeeze out as much water as possible. Remove a third of the spinach and purée in a food processor with 1 tablespoon of water. Set the purée aside until you are ready to cook the crêpes.

Finely chop the remaining spinach and mix together with the ricotta. Season with salt and pepper, nutmeg and the lemon juice and zest. Fold in the Parmesan then store in the refrigerator.

To make the crêpe batter, put the flour, water, eggs and reserved spinach purée into a large mixing bowl. Season with salt and pepper and whisk until you have a smooth and runny batter. Cover and put the batter in the refrigerator to rest for 30 minutes.

When you are ready to serve, remove the batter from the refrigerator and stir gently. Put a little butter in a large frying pan/skillet set over medium heat. Allow the butter to melt and coat the base of the pan, then ladle a spoonful of the rested batter into the pan and quickly spread the batter out very thinly. You can do this either by tilting the pan, or, for best results, use a crêpe swizzle stick. Cook until the top of the pancake is set then turn over carefully with a spatula and cook on the other side for a further 1–2 minutes until the crêpe is crispy. Keep the crêpes warm while you cook the remaining batter.

Put some of the chilled ricotta filling in the centre of each crêpe and roll up to serve. Top with a little extra grated Parmesan if desired.

Ham and Emmental crêpes

Ham and cheese crêpes are a very popular lunch in France. These are filled with a delicate béchamel sauce and ham, rolled up and topped with grated cheese which melts when they are baked in the oven. Be careful of the oozing cheese when plating up!

140 g/1 cup plain/
   all-purpose flour
1 egg and 1 yolk
30 g/2 tablespoons
   melted butter
2 teaspoons wholegrain
   mustard
300 ml/1¼ cups milk
120 g/1 cup wafer-thin
   ham
150 g/1½ cups Emmental,
   grated
sea salt flakes and freshly
   ground black pepper,
   to taste

Sauce
825 ml/3⅓ cup milk
1 small onion, peeled and
   kept whole
1 teaspoon black
   peppercorns
2 bay leaves
a pinch of freshly grated
   nutmeg
75 g/5 tablespoons butter
75 g/½ cup plain/
   all-purpose flour, sifted

*a crêpe swizzle stick
   (optional)*

SERVES 8

Begin by preparing the béchamel sauce. Put the milk in a saucepan or pot set over medium heat. Quickly add the onion, peppercorns, bay leaves and nutmeg and bring the milk to the boil. Remove from the heat and leave to infuse for 30 minutes. Strain the sauce through a sieve/strainer over a bowl and discard the onion, leaves and peppercorns. In a separate saucepan or pot set over medium heat, melt the butter until it starts to foam. Tip in all of the flour in one go, remove the pan from the heat and beat the mixture hard until the flour is incorporated and you have a thick paste which leaves the sides of the pan. Reheat the milk and add a little at a time to the flour paste, beating well over the heat as the milk is added. When all the milk is incorporated you should have a smooth white sauce. Season with salt and pepper to taste. Cover and set aside.

To make the crêpe batter, put the flour, egg and egg yolk, melted butter and mustard in a large mixing bowl. Season well with salt and pepper. Whisking all the time, gradually add the milk until you have a smooth and runny batter. Leave the batter to rest in the refrigerator for 30 minutes.

When you are ready to serve, remove the batter from the refrigerator and stir once. Put a little butter in a large frying pan/skillet set over medium heat. Allow the butter to melt and coat the base of the pan, then ladle a spoonful of the rested batter into the pan and quickly spread the batter out very thinly. You can do this either by tilting the pan, or, for best results, use a crêpe swizzle stick. Cook until the top of the pancake is set then turn over carefully with a spatula and cook on the other side for a further 1–2 minutes until the crêpe is golden brown. Keep warm while you cook the remaining batter.

Preheat the oven to 190°C (375°F) Gas 5.

Spread a generous spoonful of béchamel over each crêpe and top with a few slices of ham. Sprinkle with a little of the cheese and then roll up the crêpe. Place in the ovenproof dish and repeat with all the remaining crêpes. Pour the rest of the béchamel sauce over the pancakes and sprinkle with the remaining cheese. Bake in the preheated oven for 10–15 minutes until the cheese has melted and turns golden brown. Serve immediately.

130 g/1 cup chickpea/gram
    flour
1 teaspoon salt
½ teaspoon ground cumin
¼ teaspoon turmeric
½ can chickpeas, drained,
    rinsed and crushed with
    a fork
240 ml/1 cup milk
1 egg
1 garlic clove, crushed
freshly grated zest and juice
    of 1 lemon
a handful of chopped fresh
    herbs (coriander/cilantro,
    parsley or chives all work
    well)
1 teaspoon bicarbonate of
    soda/baking soda
250 g/9 oz. halloumi, sliced
1 tablespoon olive oil

Salsa
2 sweet red (bell) peppers,
    halved
2 sweetcorn cobs
a handful of cherry tomatoes
3 tablespoons olive oil
½ red onion, finely diced
½–1 fresh red chilli/chile,
    finely diced
a handful of fresh coriander/
    cilantro, finely chopped
freshly squeezed juice of ½
    a lime
1 teaspoon white wine
    vinegar
1 teaspoon caster/granulated
    sugar
salt and freshly ground black
    pepper

SERVES 6–8

Herby chickpea pancakes with halloumi and roasted corn salsa

Salty halloumi paired with fluffy savoury pancakes and a crunchy fresh salsa makes for brunch heaven. However, you could also serve this dish as a light lunch or supper.

Preheat the oven to 200°C (400°F) Gas 6.

To make the salsa, put the peppers in a roasting pan skin-side up, with the sweetcorn cobs and tomatoes. Sprinkle generously with salt and pepper and drizzle with 2 tablespoons olive oil. Roast in the top half of the preheated oven for 20–25 minutes until the skin of the peppers has shrivelled and the corn is golden. Reserve any juices left in the pan. Peel the skin off the peppers and remove the corn kernels from the cobs. Finely chop the peppers and break up the tomatoes with a fork, then put them in a bowl with the onion, chilli/chile and coriander/cilantro.

In a separate bowl, combine the lime juice, vinegar, sugar and remaining olive oil. Season with salt and pepper and stir until well combined. Pour over the vegetable mixture and stir.

To make the chickpea pancakes, put the chickpea/gram flour, salt and cumin and turmeric in a bowl. Stir in the crushed chickpeas.

In a separate bowl, combine the milk, egg, garlic and lemon juice and zest and beat well with a fork until well combined.

Make a well in the centre of the dry ingredients, pour in the milk mixture and stir from the centre until well combined. Add the chopped herbs, cover and set aside in the refrigerator for 20 minutes or until you are ready to cook the pancakes. Just before you make the pancakes, stir in the bicarbonate of soda/ baking soda.

Lightly grease a frying pan/skillet and set over medium–high heat. Add a ladle of batter and cook until bubbles begin to form and the pancake starts to firm up. Turn it over and cook until both sides are golden brown and it has puffed up slightly. You can keep the pancakes warm in a low oven until ready to serve.

Lightly oil the halloumi and cook over high heat on a stovetop griddle/grill pan for 1 minute on each side until golden. Put the pancakes onto serving plates, top with the salsa and serve.

Pea, basil and feta fritters with roasted tomatoes

Roasted tomatoes
300 g/2 cups cherry
tomatoes, halved
2 tablespoons olive oil
2 tablespoons balsamic
vinegar

Fritters
200 g/1⅓ cups frozen
peas, quickly defrosted
(you can use the pan
you'll fry the fritters in)
100 g/¾ cup plain/
all-purpose flour
1 teaspoon baking
powder
1 egg
150 ml/⅔ cup milk
grated zest of ½ lemon
100 g/⅔ cup crumbled
feta
30 basil leaves, torn into
small shreds
2 tablespoons olive oil
salt and black pepper
100 g/3½ oz. prosciutto,
to serve

**MAKES 12–14 FRITTERS,
OR SERVES 4 FOR
BRUNCH**

This is a dish built for a sunny weekend. Fritters hold their own both on a breakfast table and later on if someone fires up a barbecue. One way to eat them is in the morning with squashed roasted tomatoes and prosciutto, but a dipping sauce of yogurt muddled with basil and mint or an avocado purée are also worth thinking about. They freeze well and can be happily warmed in the oven or a toasted sandwich maker.

Preheat the oven to 180°C (350°F) Gas 4.

For the roasted tomatoes, put the halved cherry tomatoes on a baking sheet, drizzle with the olive oil and vinegar and sprinkle with a few pinches of salt. Roast in the oven for 25–35 minutes until the tomatoes are lightly caramelized.

For the fritters, defrost the peas over medium heat in a frying pan/skillet.

Combine the flour, baking powder, egg, milk and lemon zest in a mixing bowl. Stir in the crumbled feta, torn basil and warmed peas. Season with salt and pepper.

Heat 1 tablespoon of the olive oil in the frying pan/skillet. Spoon around 1½ tablespoons of batter per fritter into the hot pan. Cook 3 fritters at a time over medium heat until you see small holes appearing on the surface. Gently flip with a spatula and cook for 2 minutes on the other side. Transfer to somewhere warm while you make the rest.

Serve the fritters with the roasted tomatoes and prosciutto.

Pasta and Rice

Lots of varieties of cheese lend themselves perfectly to pasta
and rice, from creamy pasta bakes to velvety risottos. This is a
chapter of deliciously indulgent comfort food at its best,
ideal for cosy nights and winter suppers – think Truffle Mac
and Cheese, Creamy Orzo Pasta Bake, Parmesan and Butter
Risotto or Creamy Radicchio and Mascarpone Risotto.

Spaghetti with Gorgonzola, pecan and mascarpone sauce

The toasted pecan nuts add texture to this rich and creamy cheese sauce. Gorgonzola is a strongly flavoured blue cheese that is perfect combined with the milder mascarpone. Other blue cheeses you could use are Roquefort or even Stilton.

450 g/1 lb. dried
   spaghetti
25 g/2 tablespoons
   unsalted butter
1 garlic clove, crushed
175 g/6 oz. Gorgonzola,
   crumbled
175 g/¾ cup mascarpone
a pinch of ground mace or
   a little freshly grated
   nutmeg
100 g/⅔ cup pecan nuts,
   toasted and roughly
   chopped
2 tablespoons freshly
   chopped chives
salt and freshly ground
   black pepper

SERVES 4

Cook the spaghetti according to the package instructions.

Meanwhile, melt the butter in a saucepan and gently fry the garlic over low heat for 2–3 minutes, or until soft but not browned. Stir in the Gorgonzola, mascarpone, mace or nutmeg along with some salt and pepper. Cook gently until the sauce is heated through but the cheese still has a little texture.

Remove the pan from the heat and stir in the pecan nuts and chives. Season to taste, then add the cooked spaghetti and mix thoroughly. Serve immediately.

Creamy orzo pasta bake

There is something very pleasing about the texture of orzo pasta and it marries well with the courgette/zucchini. This dish is ideal for a crowd and can be a meal in itself, or accompany it with a mixed bean salad. Alternatively, stir in a drained can of haricot/navy beans or chickpeas and serve with a fresh tomato salad for a nutritious supper.

250 g/2 cups orzo (rice-
    shaped pasta)
400 ml/1⅔ cups double/
    heavy cream or crème
    fraîche
1 courgette/zucchini,
    roughly grated
a large handful of freshly
    chopped flat-leaf
    parsley leaves
    (optional)
finely grated zest of
    ½ lemon
50 g/½ cup grated hard
    cheese, such as cheddar
    or Emmental, or
    crumbled feta
salt and freshly ground
    black pepper

*a 30 x 20-cm/12 x 8-inch
    ovenproof baking dish,
    greased or buttered*

MAKES 6–8 SERVINGS

Preheat the oven to 200°C (400°F) Gas 6.

Cook the orzo according to the package instructions, drain well and transfer to a mixing bowl. Pour in the cream or crème fraîche and add the courgette/zucchini, parsley (if using) and lemon zest. Mix well until thoroughly combined. Season well and transfer to the prepared baking dish. Spread evenly and sprinkle over the cheese.

Bake in the preheated oven for about 20–30 minutes, until just browned, then serve immediately.

Provençal tomato and goat's cheese pasta gratin

A taste trio that sings of Mediterranean sunshine, this mac and cheese melange of sliced goat's cheese, thyme-scented cherry tomatoes and fresh basil will transport you straight to the Côte d'Azur. Serve with a crisp green salad dressed with vinaigrette and a chilled bottle of rosé from Provence.

500 g/1 lb. macaroni

500 g/1 lb. cherry tomatoes, halved

a small head of garlic, cloves separated but skins left on

leaves from a few sprigs of thyme, freshly chopped

2–3 tablespoons extra virgin olive oil

600 ml/2½ cups double/ heavy cream

leaves from a small bunch of fresh basil, thinly sliced

100 g/1¼ cups grated hard goat's cheese

2 x 60 g/2 oz. Crottin de Chavignol or other mild goat's cheese, ends trimmed and sliced

50 g/1 cup fresh breadcrumbs

salt and freshly ground black pepper

SERVES 6–8

Cook the macaroni according to the package instructions.

Preheat the oven to 190°C (375°F) Gas 5.

Arrange the halved tomatoes and garlic in a single layer on a baking sheet; some skin-side up and some not. Sprinkle over the thyme and oil and toss to coat lightly. Roast in the oven for 15–20 minutes until just charred.

Remove the tomatoes and garlic from the oven, slip the garlic cloves out of their skins and chop finely. Set aside. Transfer the tomatoes to a very large bowl and season lightly with salt. Set aside.

Preheat the grill/broiler to medium–hot.

Put the cream in a large saucepan and bring just to the boil, stirring occasionally. Add the basil, chopped garlic and a good pinch of salt, then reduce the heat. Add the grated hard goat's cheese and stir well to melt.

Put the cooked macaroni in the bowl with the tomatoes. Pour over the hot cream sauce and mix well. Taste and adjust the seasoning. Transfer the macaroni mixture to a baking dish and spread evenly. Top with a good grinding of black pepper and arrange the Crottin de Chavignol slices on top of the macaroni. Sprinkle with the breadcrumbs and grill/broil for 5–10 minutes until the top is crunchy and golden brown.

Serve immediately.

Artichoke, mushroom and olive pasta bake with provolone

2–3 tablespoons olive oil
1 onion, finely chopped
½ teaspoon dried oregano
½ teaspoon dried thyme
130 g/2 cups coarsely chopped white mushrooms
4 garlic cloves, crushed
¼ teaspoon chilli flakes/ hot pepper flakes
125 ml/½ cup dry white or red wine
2 x 400-g/14-oz. cans chopped tomatoes
400-g/14-oz. can artichoke hearts, drained and sliced
50 g/½ cup stoned/pitted black olives, sliced
a pinch of sugar
400 g/14 oz. dried tube pasta, such as penne or rigatoni
150 g/5½ oz. provolone, cubed

Béchamel sauce
50 g/3½ tablespoons unsalted butter
35 g/¼ cup plain/ all-purpose flour
600 ml/2½ cups hot milk
3–4 tablespoons freshly grated Parmesan
sea salt flakes and freshly ground black pepper

a 30 x 20-cm/12 x 8-in. baking dish, greased

SERVES 4

Here is a great vegetarian dish, with so much flavour no one will miss the meat! This recipe calls for provolone which is a smoked Italian cheese, but almost any cheese can be used so experiment with different types – Gruyère is a great one here, as is smoked mozzarella, soft goat's cheese or even mature Cheddar. Serve with a crisp green salad.

Heat 1 tablespoon of the oil in a large frying pan/skillet. Add the onion and cook over low heat for about 5 minutes, until soft. Stir in the oregano, thyme and mushrooms and cook for 2–3 minutes more, adding a little more oil if required.

Stir in the garlic and chilli flakes/hot pepper flakes and season with salt. Cook for 1 minute, then add the wine. Cook for 1 minute more, then add the tomatoes, artichokes and olives. Add the sugar, season, stir to combine and simmer for about 15 minutes. Taste and adjust the seasoning if necessary.

Preheat the oven to 200°C (400°F) Gas 6.

To prepare the béchamel sauce, melt the butter in a heavy-based saucepan set over low heat. Add the flour and cook, stirring, for 1 minute. Slowly pour in the hot milk, whisking continuously, and simmer until the mixture thickens. Season well. Stir in 2 tablespoons of the Parmesan and set aside.

Cook the pasta according the package instructions until just al dente. Drain and set aside.

To assemble, spread a small amount of the tomato mixture over the bottom of the baking dish and add 1 tablespoon of the oil. Arrange about one-third of the cooked pasta in a single layer on the bottom. Top with half of the remaining tomato mixture and spread evenly. Cover with another layer of pasta (using half of the remaining amount). Spoon over half of the béchamel and spread evenly. Top with the provolone, spacing the pieces evenly. Spoon the remaining tomato mixture on top. Top with the remaining pasta and béchamel. Sprinkle with the remaining Parmesan. Bake in the preheated oven for about 30–40 minutes, until browned. Serve immediately.

Shrimp and feta macaroni

Inspired by a traditional Greek dish, this is simple yet elegant and as good for a quick midweek supper as it is for impressive entertaining.

500 g/1 lb. macaroni

2–3 tablespoons
vegetable oil

1 large onion, finely diced

350 g/12 oz. raw prawns/
shrimp

1 teaspoon dried thyme

1 teaspoon dried oregano

2 garlic cloves, crushed

1 x 400-g/14-oz. can
chopped tomatoes

100 g/⅔ cup crumbled
feta

50 g/1 cup fresh
breadcrumbs

salt and freshly ground
black pepper

Béchamel sauce

50 g/3½ tablespoons
unsalted butter

60 g/6 tablespoons
plain/all-purpose flour

625 ml/2½ cups milk

1 teaspoon salt

100 g/1¼ cups grated
Graviera or Kasseri

200 g/1⅔ cups grated
Cheddar

SERVES 6–8

Cook the macaroni according to the package instructions.

Heat the oil in a large sauté pan with a lid. Add the onion and cook over medium heat for 5 minutes until just golden. Stir in the prawns/shrimp, thyme, oregano and ½ teaspoon salt, and cook until the prawns/shrimp just turn pink. Add the garlic and cook gently for 1 minute, taking care not to let it burn. Add the tomatoes and a grinding of black pepper and simmer very gently for about 15–30 minutes until the mixture has reduced to a jam-like consistency.

Preheat the grill/broiler to medium.

To make the béchamel sauce, melt the butter in a saucepan. Stir in the flour and cook, stirring constantly, for 1 minute. Pour in the milk in a steady stream, whisking constantly, and continue to whisk for 3–5 minutes until the sauce begins to thicken. Season with salt. Remove from the heat and add the cheeses, mixing well with a spoon to incorporate. Taste and adjust the seasoning.

Put the cooked macaroni in a large mixing bowl. Pour over the hot béchamel sauce and mix well. Taste the prawn/shrimp mixture and adjust the seasoning as necessary. Add to the macaroni and mix well. Transfer the macaroni mixture to a baking dish (or to individual baking dishes) and spread evenly. Sprinkle over the feta and scatter the breadcrumbs evenly over the top. Grill/broil for 5–10 minutes until the top is crunchy and golden brown. Serve immediately.

Truffle mac and cheese

In order to get the best results from this gourmet recipe, the key is to use the highest-quality cheeses you can find. Choose a good mature/sharp Cheddar, Parmesan and another flavoursome hard cheese such as Lincolnshire Poacher or Gruyère.

500 g/1 lb. macaroni

1 preserved truffle, finely chopped (reserving 3 slices to decorate)

50 g/1 cup fresh breadcrumbs

fine sea salt flakes and freshly ground black pepper

Béchamel sauce

50 g/3½ tablespoons unsalted butter

60 g/6 tablespoons plain/all-purpose flour

625 ml/2½ cups milk

1 teaspoon salt

100 g/¾ cup grated mature/sharp Cheddar

100 g/¾ cup grated Lincolnshire Poacher or Gruyère

100 g/1¼ cups Parmesan

2 tablespoons truffle paste or truffle oil

SERVES 6–8

Cook the macaroni according to the package instructions.

Preheat the grill/broiler to medium–hot.

To make the béchamel sauce, melt the butter in a saucepan. Stir in the flour and cook, stirring constantly, for 1 minute. Pour in the milk in a steady stream, whisking constantly, and continue to whisk for 3–5 minutes until the sauce begins to thicken. Season with salt. Remove from the heat and add the cheeses and truffle paste or truffle oil, mixing well with a spoon to incorporate. Taste and adjust the seasoning.

Put the cooked macaroni in a large mixing bowl. Stir in the chopped truffle, pour over the hot béchamel sauce and mix well. Taste and adjust the seasoning. Transfer the macaroni mixture to a baking dish and spread evenly. Top with a good grinding of black pepper and sprinkle the breadcrumbs evenly over the top. Decorate with the reserved truffle slices. Grill/broil for 5–10 minutes until the top is crunchy and golden brown. Serve immediately.

250-g/9-oz. tub ricotta

180 g/1½ cups chopped frozen spinach, defrosted

1 egg

4 tablespoons finely grated Parmesan (or vegetarian Italian-style hard cheese if cooking for vegetarians)

1 x 300-g/10½-oz. package fresh lasagne sheets (minimum 8 slices)

80–100 g/½–1 cup grated Cheddar

2 x 125-g/4½-oz. balls mozzarella, sliced

salt and freshly ground black pepper

Vegetable bolognese

250 g/2½ cups coarsely chopped mushrooms

1 onion, coarsely chopped

1 carrot, coarsely chopped

1 small leek, washed

2 garlic cloves

1 celery stick, chopped

2–3 tablespoons extra virgin olive oil

1 teaspoon dried thyme

700 ml/2¾ cups passata/ strained tomatoes

400-g/14-oz. can chopped tomatoes

a pinch of sugar

1 dried bay leaf

salt and freshly ground black pepper

a 20 x 25 cm/8 x 10-in. lasagne dish

MAKES 6–8 SERVINGS

Three-cheese vegetable lasagne

Here is an indulgent supper dish all the family can enjoy. Putting the vegetables for the sauce in the food processor gives this vegetable-laden sauce a pleasing texture as well as disguising the fact that there are a good few vegetables included.

To make the vegetable bolognese, put the mushrooms, onion, carrot, leek, garlic and celery in a food processor and process until very finely chopped. Transfer to a frying pan/skillet. Add the oil and thyme and cook over medium heat for 3–5 minutes, stirring often, until just beginning to brown. Add the passata/ strained tomatoes, chopped tomatoes, sugar and bay leaf. Stir to blend, then simmer, uncovered, for at least 15 minutes. Season to taste.

Preheat the oven to 200°C (400°F) Gas 6.

Put the ricotta, spinach, egg, Parmesan and a good pinch each of salt and pepper in a mixing bowl and whisk until thoroughly blended.

Spread a thin layer of the vegetable bolognese in the bottom of the lasagne dish and drizzle with a little olive oil. Top with two sheets of lasagne. Spread with just under one-third of the bolognese and top with two more lasagne sheets. Spread half of the ricotta mixture on top and sprinkle with half the grated Cheddar. Top with two lasagne sheets then spread with one-third of the remaining bolognese. Top with two more lasagne sheets, spread over the remaining ricotta mixture and sprinkle over the remaining Cheddar. Top with the remaining lasagne sheets and spread with a good layer of the bolognese.

Arrange the mozzarella slices on top and bake in the preheated oven for about 30–40 minutes, until browned and bubbling. Serve hot with a salad.

Jalapeño, tomato and Monterey Jack pasta bake

Cheese and chilli/chile are time-honoured companions and this recipe carries on the tradition. This delicious dish is quick to prepare and is perfect for a late-night supper or weekend brunch.

500 g/1 lb. macaroni

80 g/1 x 3-oz. can jalapeños, chopped

300 g/10 oz. cherry tomatoes, chopped

a few sprigs of coriander/cilantro, freshly chopped

50 g/1 cup fresh breadcrumbs

fine sea salt flakes and freshly ground black pepper

Béchamel sauce

50 g/3½ tablespoons unsalted butter

60 g/6 tablespoons plain/all-purpose flour

625 ml/2½ cups milk

1 teaspoon salt

200 g/1⅔ cups grated Monterey Jack

100 g/¾ cup grated Cheddar

SERVES 6–8

Cook the macaroni according to the package instructions.

Preheat the grill/broiler to medium–hot.

To make the béchamel sauce, melt the butter in a saucepan. Stir in the flour and cook, stirring constantly, for 1 minute. Pour in the milk in a steady stream, whisking constantly, and continue to whisk for 3–5 minutes until the sauce begins to thicken. Season with salt. Remove from the heat and add the cheeses, mixing well with a spoon to incorporate. Taste and adjust the seasoning.

Put the cooked macaroni in a large mixing bowl. Add the jalapeños, tomatoes and coriander/cilantro. Pour over the hot béchamel sauce and mix well. Taste and adjust the seasoning. Transfer the macaroni mixture to a baking dish and spread evenly. Top with a good grinding of black pepper and sprinkle the breadcrumbs evenly over the top. Grill/broil for 5–10 minutes until the top is crunchy and golden brown. Serve immediately.

Parmesan and butter risotto

When you have nothing except risotto rice in the cupboard, and a chunk of Parmesan and some butter in the refrigerator, yet feel the need for comfort and luxury, this is the risotto for you. It is pale, golden, smooth and creamy and relies totally on the quality of the rice, butter and cheese. Use real Parmigiano Reggiano, with its sweet, nutty flavour, and nothing else.

about 1.5 litres/6 cups hot vegetable or chicken stock

150 g/1 stick plus 3 tablespoons unsalted butter

1 onion, finely chopped

500 g/2⅓ cups risotto rice, preferably carnaroli

150 ml/⅔ cup dry white wine

100 g/1 cup grated Parmesan, plus extra to serve

salt and freshly ground black pepper

SERVES 4–6

Put the stock in a saucepan and keep at a gentle simmer. Melt half the butter in a large, heavy saucepan and add the onion. Cook gently for 10 minutes until soft, golden and translucent but not browned. Add the rice and stir until well coated with the butter and heated through. Pour in the wine and boil hard until it has reduced and almost disappeared. This will remove any raw alcohol taste.

Begin adding the stock, a large ladleful at a time, stirring gently until each ladleful has almost been absorbed by the rice. The risotto should be kept at a bare simmer throughout cooking, so don't let the rice dry out – add more stock as necessary. Continue until the rice is tender and creamy, but the grains still firm. (This should take 15–20 minutes depending on the type of rice used.)

Taste and season well with salt and pepper, then stir in the remaining butter and all the Parmesan. Cover and let rest for a couple of minutes so the risotto can relax and the cheese melt, then serve immediately with extra grated Parmesan. You may like to add a little more stock just before you serve, but don't let the risotto wait around too long or the rice will turn mushy.

Artichoke and pecorino risotto

Smoky chargrilled artichokes are wonderful combined with nutty pecorino. Pecorino is made from sheep's milk (latte de pecora) and when aged can be grated like Parmesan.

12 fresh artichokes, or 12 chargrilled deli artichokes, or 8 frozen artichoke bottoms, thawed

about 1.5 litres/6 cups hot vegetable or chicken stock

125 g/1 stick unsalted butter, plus extra for sautéing

1 onion, finely chopped

500 g/2⅓ cups risotto rice

150 ml/⅔ cup dry white wine

75 g/¾ cup grated pecorino, plus extra to serve

salt and freshly ground black pepper

SERVES 4

First prepare the fresh artichokes, if using (see below), then brush with olive oil and chargrill for 5 minutes on a stove-top grill pan, turning often. If using chargrilled ones from the deli, cut them in quarters and set aside. If using thawed frozen ones, slice them and fry in a little butter until golden.

Put the stock in a saucepan and keep at a gentle simmer. Melt half the butter in a large, heavy saucepan and add the onion. Cook gently for 10 minutes until soft, golden and translucent but not browned. Add the rice and stir until well coated with the butter and heated through. Pour in the wine and boil hard until it has reduced and almost disappeared.

Begin adding the stock, a large ladleful at a time, stirring gently until each ladleful has almost been absorbed by the rice. Continue until the rice is tender and creamy, but the grains still firm. (This should take 15–20 minutes depending on the type of rice used.) Taste, season well and beat in the remaining butter and all the pecorino. Fold in the artichokes. Cover and let rest for a couple of minutes so the risotto can relax, then serve immediately with extra grated pecorino.

NOTE: To prepare fresh young artichokes, you will need 1 fresh lemon, halved, and purple-green baby artichokes with stems and heads, about 10 cm/4 in. long. Fill a large bowl with water and squeeze in the juice of ½ lemon to acidulate it. Use the other lemon half to rub the cut portions of the artichoke as you work. Trim the artichokes by snapping off the dark outer leaves, starting at the base. Trim the stalk down to 5 cm/2 in. Trim away the green outer layer at the base and peel the fibrous outside of the stalk with a vegetable peeler. Cut about 1 cm/½ in. off the tip of each artichoke heart. Put each artichoke in the lemony water until needed, as this will stop them discolouring. Drain and use as required.

Creamy radicchio and mascarpone risotto

Here is a dish from the Veneto, where vialone nano rice is grown, as well as several varieties of radicchio. Stirring in a good spoonful of mascarpone or cream at the end enriches the risotto and adds sweetness. The risotto has both a sweet and a bitter flavour. Add a few currants plumped up for 20 minutes in warm grappa for an added surprise.

about 1.5 litres/6 cups hot
    vegetable or chicken
    stock
125 g/1 stick unsalted
    butter
2 carrots, finely diced
125 g/½ cup finely diced
    smoked pancetta
2 garlic cloves, finely
    chopped
500 g/1 lb. radicchio,
    finely shredded
500 g/2⅓ cups risotto rice
2 tablespoons currants
    soaked in 4 tablespoons
    warm grappa for
    20 minutes (optional)
3 tablespoons
    mascarpone or
    double/heavy cream
75 g/¾ cup grated
    Parmesan, plus extra
    to serve
salt and freshly ground
    black pepper

SERVES 6

Put the stock in a saucepan and keep at a gentle simmer. Melt half the butter in a large, heavy saucepan and add the carrots. Cook gently for 5 minutes until softening. Add the pancetta and garlic, and cook for 4 minutes until just beginning to colour. Stir in the radicchio and cook for 5 minutes until it begins to wilt.

Add the rice and stir until heated through. Add a ladleful of hot stock and simmer, stirring until absorbed. Continue adding the stock ladle by ladle, making sure the rice is never dry, until all the stock is absorbed. The rice should be tender and creamy but still have some bite to it. (This should take 15–20 minutes depending on the type of rice used.)

Taste and season well with salt and plenty of freshly ground black pepper. Add the grappa-soaked currants, if using, and stir in the remaining butter, the mascarpone or cream and the Parmesan. Cover and let rest for a couple of minutes so the risotto can relax, then serve immediately with extra grated Parmesan.

Breads and Small Bakes

Feta cheese makes a wonderful addition to cornbread, as it adds a tang of flavour and pops of white colour, which stand out against the yellow bread. Savoury muffins, scones and biscuits also work well with the rich addition of grated hard cheeses such as Parmesan, which pack a lot of flavour.

Spicy feta cornbread

260 g/1⅔ cups polenta/
   cornmeal
75 g/scant ⅔ cup plain/
   all-purpose flour
1½ teaspoons baking
   powder
1 teaspoon salt
1 teaspoon caster/
   superfine sugar
100 g/scant ½ cup light
   brown soft sugar
1 egg
360 ml/1⅓ cups milk
5 tablespoons vegetable
   oil
1 roasted red (bell)
   pepper, diced
kernels from 1 cooked
   corn cob or 180 g/
   ⅔ cup canned or frozen
   sweetcorn kernels
1 fresh red chilli/chile,
   finely diced
2 teaspoons chilli flakes/
   hot pepper flakes
1½ tablespoons parsley,
   freshly chopped
30 g/1 oz. feta or goat's
   cheese, crumbled
butter or cream cheese,
   to serve (optional)

*a 900-g/2-lb. loaf pan, lined
   with parchment paper*

SERVES 4–6

There are lots of different ways to make cornbread and many different ingredients you can add to it. This is a basic recipe, which uses tasty feta or goat's cheese, but you can experiment with other cheeses, too.

Preheat the oven to 200°C (400°F) Gas 6.

Put the polenta/cornmeal, flour, baking powder, salt and sugars in a mixing bowl and stir to combine. In a separate bowl, combine the egg, milk and oil and whisk lightly. Make a well in the centre of the dry ingredients. Pour in the egg mixture and stir to combine.

Add the red pepper, corn, chilli/chile, chilli flakes/hot pepper flakes, parsley and cheese and mix well.

Pour the mixture into the prepared loaf pan and bake in the middle of the preheated oven for 25–30 minutes, until a skewer inserted into the middle comes out clean.

Cut into slices and serve as they are or spread with butter or cream cheese, if liked. This cornbread is also delicious served with scrambled eggs.

Lemon thyme and feta loaf

This is a cross between a savoury bread and a cake. It rises with baking powder a bit like soda bread, so it's really simple to prepare. It's great on a hot day with gazpacho or on a cold evening slathered with butter and served with a warming spicy soup.

325 g/2½ cups plain/
all-purpose flour
2 tablespoons baking
powder
1 teaspoon salt
200 ml/⅔ cup plus 2
tablespoons whole milk
150 ml/⅔ cup extra virgin
olive oil
2 eggs, beaten
1 large courgette/
zucchini, coarsely
grated
125 g/1¼ cups crumbled
feta
leaves from 2 lemon
thyme sprigs
freshly ground black
pepper

*a 900-g/2-lb. loaf pan, lined
with parchment paper*

SERVES 4–6

Preheat the oven to 180°C (350°F) Gas 4.

Sift the flour, baking powder and salt into a large bowl and season with freshly ground black pepper.

In a measuring jug/cup, combine the milk and olive oil and beat in the eggs. Stir into the dry ingredients along with the courgette/zucchini, two-thirds of the feta and half the thyme leaves. Stir until there are no more floury pockets but don't overbeat it or you'll make the mixture tough. Spoon into the prepared loaf pan. Scatter over the remaining feta and remaining thyme. Bake in the preheated oven for 1–1¼ hours, or until a skewer inserted in the centre comes out clean.

Remove the pan from the oven and leave to cool for 10 minutes in the pan, then turn out onto a wire rack to cool completely.

Parmesan buttermilk scones

Buttermilk makes for wonderfully light scones. Here, Parmesan cheese is used to give a subtle, rich cheesy flavour to savoury scones.

**250 g/2 cups self-raising/
  self-rising flour**
**1 teaspoon baking
  powder**
**50 g/3 tablespoons
  butter, diced**
**50 g/⅔ cup finely grated
  Parmesan, plus extra
  for topping**
1 egg
**125 ml/½ cup buttermilk,
  plus extra for glazing**
salt

*6-cm/2½-in. diameter
  cookie cutter*
a baking sheet, greased

MAKES 8

Preheat the oven to 220°C (425°F) Gas 7.

Sift the flour, baking powder and a pinch of salt into a large mixing bowl. Next, rub in the butter with your fingertips until it is absorbed into the mixture. Stir in the grated Parmesan and mix well.

In a separate bowl, use a fork to lightly whisk together the egg and buttermilk. Now add it to the flour mixture and lightly fold it in to form a soft, sticky dough.

Roll the dough out on a lightly floured work surface to 2.5 cm/1 in. thickness and use the cookie cutter to cut out 8 scones.

Place the scones on the prepared baking sheet. Brush each scone with a little buttermilk and sprinkle with a little grated Parmesan.

Bake in the preheated oven for 10–15 minutes until they have risen and are golden brown. These are particularly good eaten warm from the oven, sliced in half with a little butter.

Blush tomato and feta muffins

Who doesn't love a savoury muffin? These combine the rich, crumbly texture of feta cheese with the sweet, ripened flavour of sun-blush tomatoes. Enjoy for breakfast, brunch, lunch or dinner alongside soups or other hot meals.

75 g/5 tablespoons butter, melted

2 eggs

140 ml/²⁄₃ cup whole milk

300 g/2⅓ cups self-raising/self-rising flour

1 teaspoon baking powder

1 teaspoon salt

2–3 pinches of dried oregano

14 sun-blush tomatoes, chopped

100 g/3½ oz. feta cheese, diced

2 x 6-hole muffin pans, lined with 10 muffin cases

MAKES 10

Preheat the oven to 200°C (400°F) Gas 6.

Whisk together the melted butter, eggs and milk in a large mixing bowl.

In a separate bowl, sift the flour and baking powder together, then stir in the salt and oregano. Pour in the melted butter mixture and quickly and lightly fold into the flour. Stir through the tomatoes and feta. Divide the mixture evenly between the muffin cases.

Bake in the preheated oven for 20–25 minutes until risen and golden brown. Serve warm from the oven or at room temperature.

Parmesan and Marcona almond biscuits

These are amazing little bite-size biscuits to serve with drinks. Don't go too mad with the chilli flakes/hot pepper flakes though – one man's mild is another man's furnace! You can freeze the dough, which makes it easy to rustle up a batch when friends call round and the wine comes out. Try to use the big, buttery Spanish Marcona almonds – they have such a special flavour.

180 g/1½ sticks butter, softened
100 g/1⅓ cups finely grated Parmesan
80 g/1 cup finely grated mature/sharp Cheddar
180 g/1⅓ cups plain/all-purpose flour
a pinch of chilli flakes/hot pepper flakes
180 g/1¼ cups roasted Marcona almonds, roughly chopped
salt

a baking sheet lined with parchment paper

MAKES ABOUT 25

Beat the butter and cheeses together in a large mixing bowl. Combine the flour, chilli flakes/hot pepper flakes and a pinch of salt in a separate bowl and work into the butter mixture to form a smooth dough. Add the almonds and work again until they are evenly incorporated.

Lay a piece of clingfilm/plastic wrap on a clean work surface. Lightly dust it with flour. Divide the mixture into two or three pieces and roll into long sausage shapes, about 2.5 cm/1 in. in diameter. Wrap them tightly in the clingfilm/plastic wrap and twist the ends to seal. Refrigerate for 15 minutes or so, until the dough has firmed up a little.

Preheat the oven to 180°C (350°F) Gas 4.

Unwrap the dough and cut into 3 mm/⅛ in. thick slices. Lay on the prepared baking sheets and bake in the preheated oven for about 6–8 minutes, until golden and firm.

Cool on a wire rack, store in an airtight container and eat within 5 days.

Blue cheese and walnut biscuits

These tasty, crumbly little treats make great pre-dinner nibbles. Freshly chopped chives make a lovely addition to the recipe, too.

90 g/6 tablespoons butter, softened

130 g/4½ oz. strong blue cheese, such as Roquefort

200 g/1⅔ cups plain/all-purpose flour

50 g/⅓ cup walnuts, chopped

salt

2 baking sheets lined with parchment paper

MAKES ABOUT 30

Preheat the oven to 180°C (350°F) Gas 4.

Beat the butter and blue cheese together in a large mixing bowl until evenly mixed. Work in the flour and a pinch of salt and bring the mixture together to form a smooth dough. Add the chopped walnuts and knead very lightly until they have all been evenly combined.

Form the mixture into two long sausage shapes and wrap both tightly in clingfilm/plastic wrap. Refrigerate for 30 minutes or so to firm up.

Unwrap the dough and cut into slices just under 1 cm/⅜ in. thick. Arrange on the prepared baking sheets, leaving a little space for spreading between each one.

Bake in the preheated oven for 10–12 minutes, until crisp and golden.

Leave to cool for 5 minutes or so, before transferring to a wire rack to cool completely. Store in an airtight container and eat within 5 days.

Desserts

Cheesecake is a favourite dessert all around the globe and it can be made using many types of cheese, from ricotta and mascarpone to cream cheese and quark. However, there are also plenty of other sweet treats that can be made with cheese, such as deep-fried fritters and stuffed French toast.

Greek baklava cheesecake

9 large sheets filo/phyllo
pastry (about 400 g/
14 oz.)
115 g/1 stick butter,
melted
3–4 tablespoons runny
Greek honey
pistachios, for sprinkling

Cheesecake filling
225 g/1 cup quark
150 g/⅔ cup cream
cheese
1 small egg, plus 1 egg
yolk
50 g/¼ cup caster/
granulated sugar
grated zest of 1 lemon
75 g/¾ cup ground
almonds

Nut filling
100 g/¾ cup pistachios
50 g/¼ cup caster/
granulated sugar, plus
extra for sprinkling
2 teaspoons ground
cinnamon

*a piping/pastry bag fitted
with a large round
nozzle/tip*
*a 23-cm/9-inch round
springform cake pan or
tarte tatin pan, greased
and lined*

SERVES 10

Baklava is not difficult to prepare and the end result is a delicious syrupy buttery pastry which is perfect with a mug of strong coffee. Its sweet, sticky and crispy consistency works perfectly with the cool creaminess of a lemony cheesecake filling. All it needs is the crunch of cinnamon nuts to finish it off.

Preheat the oven to 180°C (350°F) Gas 4.

To prepare the cheesecake filling, whisk together the quark, cream cheese, egg and egg yolk, sugar, lemon zest and almonds in a large mixing bowl until the mixture is smooth and creamy. Spoon the mixture into the piping/pastry bag.

For the nut filling, blitz the pistachios with the sugar and cinnamon in a food processor until finely chopped.

Remove the filo/phyllo pastry from the packet and cut the sheets in half so that you are left with 18 smaller sheets. Cover with a damp kitchen cloth, which will prevent it from drying out and cracking. Lay one sheet of filo/phyllo on a clean work surface and brush with the melted butter using a pastry brush. Cover with a second sheet of filo/phyllo and brush with butter again. Sprinkle with a few tablespoons of the nut mixture so that the whole sheet is covered in a thin layer of nuts, then cover with a third sheet of filo/phyllo and brush again with butter. Pipe a line of the cheesecake filling along one of the long edges, then roll up so that the filling is in the middle of each tube.

Place the filo/phyllo tube around the edge of the prepared cake pan. Repeat with the remaining pastry until you have made 6 tubes of cheesecake pastry in total. Continue to arrange them in the pan in a spiral so that the ends of each tube touch, then brush the top of the pastry with a little more butter and bake in the preheated oven for 20–30 minutes until the top of the pastry is crisp and golden.

Heat the honey in a saucepan until it becomes thin and easily pourable then spoon over the baklava and leave to cool completely. Sprinkle with bright green pistachios and a little sugar, to serve.

Polish cheesecake

Pastry

125 g/1 stick butter, chilled

230 g/1¾ cups plain/ all-purpose flour

50 g/¼ cup caster/ granulated sugar

2 egg yolks

1 tablespoon cream cheese

a splash of milk, to glaze

Filling

500 g/generous 2 cups twaróg cheese

250 g/generous 1 cup cream cheese

4 eggs

400 g/1¾ cups condensed milk

125 g/9 tablespoons butter, melted

icing/confectioners' sugar, for dusting

a deep 30 x 22-cm/12 x 9-in. roasting pan, greased
leaf pastry cutters

SERVES 14

Twaróg cheese is a traditional Polish cheese, somewhat similar to cottage cheese. You need to pass it through a sieve/strainer before using otherwise the cheesecake will have a grainy texture. Twaróg cheese has a distinct sharp flavour with hints of lemon so no additional flavouring is used in this cheesecake, but you could add berries, lemon zest or vanilla, if you wish. If you are short of time, you could use 375 g/14 oz. ready-made sweet shortcrust pastry.

For the pastry crust, rub the butter into the flour until it resembles fine breadcrumbs. Add the sugar, egg yolks and cream cheese and mix together to a soft dough with your fingers, adding a little extra flour if the mixture is too sticky, or a little chilled water if it is too dry. Wrap the pastry dough in cling film/plastic wrap and chill in the refrigerator for 1 hour.

Bring the dough back to room temperature and, on a lightly floured surface, roll it out to a sheet large enough to line the roasting pan. Lay the pastry into the prepared pan and trim the edges. Roll out the trimmings and cut out small leaf shapes with which to decorate the cheesecake.

Preheat the oven to 170°C (325°F) Gas 3.

To make the filling, pass the twaróg cheese through a fine mesh sieve/strainer. In a large mixing bowl, whisk the strained twaróg, cream cheese, eggs and condensed milk together until you have a smooth cream. Slowly pour in the melted butter, whisking all the time. Pour the mixture into the pastry case, arrange the pastry leaves on top. Brush the leaves with a little milk, to glaze, then bake in the preheated oven for 45–60 minutes until the cheesecake is golden brown and still wobbles slightly in the centre. Remove from the oven and leave to cool, then chill in the refrigerator before serving.

To serve, cut the cheesecake into squares and dust with icing/confectioners' sugar.

Fig and honey ricotta cheesecake

Ricotta makes for a pleasantly light-textured cheesecake. Here it's combined with figs and honey to give a Mediterranean flavour. Serve it for dessert or enjoy it with coffee as a mid-morning treat.

150 g/5 oz. digestive biscuits or graham crackers

50 g/3½ tablespoons butter, melted

750 g/3 cups ricotta

2 eggs

2 tablespoons runny honey

½ teaspoon orange flower water

40 g/⅓ cup plain/ all-purpose flour

5–6 fresh figs, halved

a 20-cm/8-in. loose-based cake pan

SERVES 6

Preheat the oven to 180°C (350°F) Gas 4.

Using a rolling pin, crush the biscuits into crumbs. Use a large bowl to mix the crumbs with the melted butter. Next, press this mixture firmly and evenly into the cake pan to form a base.

In a separate large bowl, mix together the ricotta and eggs. Stir in the honey, orange flower water and flour. Spoon the ricotta mixture evenly across the base. Now, press the halved figs, skin-side down, into the ricotta mixture.

Bake the cheesecake in the preheated oven for 50–60 minutes until set. Remove the pan from the oven and cool, then cover and chill until serving.

The cheesecake will keep for a few days, covered, in the refrigerator.

Simply vanilla cheesecake

This cheesecake is simple but is always popular – no frills, no fuss, just good old-fashioned vanilla. It is delicious served with fresh berries of your choice and a little pouring cream.

Crumb case
300 g/10½ oz. digestive
   biscuits or graham
   crackers
150 g/1¼ sticks butter,
   melted

Filling
600 ml/2½ cups crème
   fraîche or sour cream
750 g/3⅓ cups cream
   cheese
4 eggs
400 g/1¾ cups condensed
   milk
2 tablespoons plain/
   all-purpose flour, sifted
1 vanilla pod/bean
fresh berries of your
   choice, to serve
pouring cream, to serve

*a 26-cm/10-in. round
   springform cake pan,
   greased and lined*

SERVES 12

Preheat the oven to 170°C (325°F) Gas 3.

To make the crumb case, crush the biscuits or graham crackers to fine crumbs in a food processor or place in a clean plastic bag and bash with a rolling pin. Transfer the crumbs to a mixing bowl and stir in the melted butter. Press the buttery crumbs into the base and sides of the prepared cake pan firmly using the back of a spoon. You need the crumbs to come up about 3–4 cm/1½ in. high on the side of the pan so that they make a case for the filling. Wrap the outside of the pan in clingfilm/plastic wrap and place in a roasting pan half full with water, ensuring that the water is not so high as to spill out. Set aside.

For the filling, whisk together the crème fraîche, cream cheese, eggs, condensed milk and flour. Using a sharp knife split the vanilla pod/bean in half, scrape out the seeds from both halves and add to the cheesecake mixture, discarding the pod/bean (see tip below). Whisk until the seeds are evenly distributed, then pour the mixture into the crumb case.

Transfer the cheesecake, in its waterbath, to the oven and bake for 1–1¼ hours until golden brown on top and still with a slight wobble in the centre. Remove the cheesecake from the waterbath and slide a knife around the edge of the pan to release the cheesecake and prevent it from cracking. Leave to cool, then transfer to the refrigerator to chill for at least 3 hours or preferably overnight. Serve with berries and pouring cream.

TIP: You can store the left over vanilla pod/bean in a jar of sugar to make vanilla sugar for baking.

Fig and ricotta pancakes with orange syrup

160 g/1¼ cups self-raising/self-rising flour, sifted

1 teaspoon baking powder

2 eggs, separated

grated zest of 2 unwaxed oranges

50 g/¼ cup caster/granulated sugar

a pinch of salt

250 ml/1 cup milk

125 g/½ cup ricotta

40 g/3 tablespoons butter, melted, plus extra for frying

4–5 ripe figs, thinly sliced

sugar nibs/pearl sugar or caster/granulated sugar, for sprinkling

Syrup

freshly squeezed juice of 4 oranges

100 g/½ cup caster/granulated sugar

50 g/3½ tablespoons butter

a large frying pan/skillet or griddle

MAKES 18

Figs are one of those fruits that always remind people of summer. They are delicious in this recipe with their vibrant pink and green colour, served drizzled with buttery orange syrup in rich pancakes laden with ricotta. Make them small enough to top with just one fig slice or make larger versions with several fig slices on top if you prefer.

Begin by preparing the syrup. Put the orange juice, sugar and butter in a saucepan or pot over medium heat and simmer until the sugar is melted. Keep the pan on the heat but turn it down to low to keep the syrup warm until ready to serve.

To make the pancake batter, put the flour, baking powder, egg yolks, orange zest, caster/granulated sugar, salt, milk and ricotta cheese in a large mixing bowl and whisk together. Add in the melted butter and whisk again. The batter should have a smooth, dropping consistency.

In a separate bowl, whisk the egg whites to stiff peaks. Gently fold the whisked egg whites into the batter mixture using a spatula. Cover and put in the refrigerator to rest for 30 minutes.

When you are ready to serve, remove the batter mixture from the refrigerator and stir once. Put a little butter in a large frying pan/skillet set over medium heat. Allow the butter to melt and coat the base of the pan, then ladle small spoonfuls of batter into the pan, leaving a little space between each. Place a slice of fig on top of each pancake and sprinkle with sugar nibs/pearl sugar or caster/granulated sugar. Cook until the underside of each pancake is golden brown and a few bubbles start to appear on the top – this will take about 1–2 minutes. Turn the pancakes over using a spatula and cook on the other side until the sugar-topped figs have caramelized and the top is golden brown. Keep the pancakes warm while you cook the remaining batter.

Serve the pancakes immediately with a drizzle of the orange syrup.

Nectarine and mascarpone-stuffed French toast

The pockets in these French toasts are filled with delicious nectarine and creamy mascarpone cheese. Served dusted with icing/confectioners' sugar and with extra fruit on the side, they are ideal for a brunch gathering with friends. Why not serve a peach bellini cocktail alongside as the perfect indulgent accompaniment?

4 thick slices of brioche

2 eggs

80 ml/scant ⅓ cup double/heavy cream

1 tablespoon caster/ granulated sugar

15–30 g/1–2 tablespoons butter, for frying

icing/confectioners' sugar, to serve

Filling

seeds of ½ vanilla pod/bean

125 g/scant 1 cup mascarpone

1 ripe nectarine or peach, stone/pit removed, diced

a large frying pan/skillet or griddle

SERVES 4

Begin by preparing the filling. Stir the vanilla seeds into the mascarpone in a mixing bowl, then add the diced nectarine.

Using a sharp knife, cut a pocket in the top of each brioche slice to create a large cavity. Take care not to cut all the way through as it is this cavity which will hold your filling. Spoon one-quarter of the nectarine mixture into each slice and press the opening down to close the pocket.

Whisk together the eggs, cream and caster/granulated sugar in a mixing bowl, transfer to a shallow dish and set aside. Melt the butter in a large frying pan/skillet set over medium heat until the butter begins to foam. Soak each sandwich in the egg mixture on one side for a few seconds, then turn over and soak the other side. The sandwiches should be fully coated in egg, but not too soggy – it is best to soak one slice at a time.

Put each sandwich straight in the hot pan before soaking and cooking the next sandwich.

Cook for 2–3 minutes on each side until the sandwiches are golden brown and the egg is cooked. Keep the cooked toast warm while you cook the remaining slices in the same way, adding a little butter to the pan each time, if required.

Cut the sandwiches in half, dust with icing/confectioners' sugar and serve immediately.

Fluffy ricotta fritters

These fluffy little morsels are made with creamy ricotta and perfect with a cup of coffee. Deep-fried snacks like these are part of Italian life and are seen as a real treat during festivals.

250 g/1 cup ricotta
2 eggs, at room temperature
2 tablespoons caster/ granulated sugar
1 teaspoon pure vanilla extract
120 g/scant 1 cup plain/ all-purpose flour
1 teaspoon baking powder
½ teaspoon salt
vegetable oil, for deep-frying
icing/confectioners' sugar, to serve

a deep-fryer
a tray lined with paper towels

SERVES 4–6

Press the ricotta through a food mill, potato ricer or sieve/strainer into a large bowl. Put the eggs, sugar and vanilla extract in a second bowl and whisk until pale and light. Fold into the ricotta.

Sift the flour with the baking powder and salt into a bowl, then fold it into the cheese and egg mixture.

Heat the vegetable oil in the deep-fryer to 190°C (375°F). Have a tray lined with paper towels and a slotted spoon or strainer at the ready.

Drop level tablespoons of the mixture into the hot oil in batches of 6. Fry for 2–3 minutes until puffed and deep brown all over (you may have to turn them in the oil). Drain and serve immediately, dusted with icing/confectioners' sugar.

Index

Recipe Credits

Belinda Williams
Pear, celery and blue cheese soup with salted sugared walnuts
Purple sprouting broccoli soup with Mrs Bells Blue
Spinach and Parmesan soup with nutmeg and rosemary
Tomato and red bell pepper soup with Wensleydale

Chloe Coker and Jane Montgomery
Breadcrumbed halloumi goujons
Butternut squash, feta and sage quiche
Herby chickpea pancakes with halloumi and roasted corn salsa
Paneer with warm curried lentil salad and a spiced dressing
Spicy feta cornbread

Fiona Beckett
Goat's cheese omelette with wild garlic/ramps and chervil
Irresistible Italian four-cheese pizza
Red bell pepper and Manchego tortilla

Hannah Miles
Courgette/zucchini and feta griddle cakes
Fig and ricotta pancakes with orange syrup
Gluten-free spinach and ricotta crêpes
Greek baklava cheesecake
Ham and Emmental crêpes
Nectarine and mascarpone stuffed French toast
Polish cheesecake
Simply vanilla cheesecake
Squash and goat's cheese pancakes
Tricolore French toast

Jenny Linford
Blush tomato and feta muffins
Cream cheese and olive parcels
Fig and honey ricotta cheesecake
Parmesan buttermilk scones
Ricotta and spinach dumplings with cherry tomato sauce
Spaghetti with Gorgonzola, pecan and mascarpone sauce

Sun-blush tomato, orange and burrata salad
Swiss chard, ricotta and pine nut/kernel tart
Tomato and ricotta roulade

Laura Washburn
Artichoke, mushroom and olive pasta bake with provolone
Balsamic mushrooms and Fontina sandwich
Blue cheese, Serrano ham and walnut pesto sandwich
Burger Scamorza
Chard and Gruyère macaroni
Chipotle, black bean and feta quesadilla with Pico de Gallo
Chorzio, Manchego and mini bell pepper sandwich
Creamy orzo pasta bake
Jalapeño, tomato and Monterey Jack pasta bake
Kimchi and Monterey jack sandwich
Lobster tail, tarragon mayonnaise and Beaufort sandwich
Provençal tomato and goat's cheese pasta gratin
Shrimp and feta macaroni
Tartiflette sandwich
Three-cheese vegetable lasagne
Truffle mac and cheese

Liz Franklin
Blue cheese and walnut biscuits
Parmesan and Marcona almond biscuits

Maxine Clark
Artichoke and pecorino risotto
Creamy radicchio and mascarpone risotto
Fluffy ricotta fritters
Goat's cheese, mushroom and rosemary pithivier
Greek spinach, feta and oregano filo pie
Parmesan and butter risotto
Pear, pecorino and Taleggio pizza with honey and sage
Pizza with artichokes and mozzarella
Potato pizza with Fontina
Ricotta and green herb torta
Ricotta, sausage and potato

pizza pie

Miisa Mink
Vegetable and blue cheese tart

Nicola Graimes
Baked goat's cheese with honey-spiced beetroot/beets
Brie, bean and crispy caper salad
Chargrilled halloumi and mint salad
Ossau iraty, asparagus and crouton salad
Pecorino, olive and parsley salad
Puy lentils, grapefruit and feta with harissa dressing
Roquefort, pecan and apple salad
Warm pearl barley, smoked cheddar and walnut salad

Ross Dobson
Asparagus, sweetcorn and goat's cheese frittata
Stuffed giant mushrooms with feta and herbs
Taleggio and potato tortilla with tapenade

Shelagh Ryan
Asparagus, goat's cheese and spinach tart
Baked ricotta with aubergine/eggplant and currant relish
Parmesan, leek and rocket/arugula and tart

Tonia George
French onion soup with Gruyère garlic toasts
Goat's cheese and anchovy palmiers
Lemon thyme and feta loaf
Tapenade with Parmesan cheese straws

Tori Haschka
Pea, basil and feta fritters with roasted tomatoes

Ursula Ferrigno
Provolone, pear and walnut salad
Sweet and sour bell peppers with mozzarella

Valerie Aikman-smith
Grilled halloumi with blistered jalapeño relish
Watermelon and ricotta salata salad with olive salt

Picture Credits

Jan Baldwin
pages 29, 43

Martin Brigdale
pages 1, 110, 143, 175-179, 183, 188

Peter Cassidy
pages 18, 44, 65, 74, 169, 181

Jonathan Gregson
page 32

Richard Jung
pages 8, 30, 84, 105-109, 113, 114, 117, 118, 121, 150

Erin Kunkel
page 17

Jason Lowe
pages 2, 155-160

David Munns
pages 64, 112

Steve Painter
pages 3, 5, 56, 59, 60, 63, 77-82, 85-98, 101, 122, 125-129, 134, 135, 140, 144, 147, 151, 152, 184, 187

William Reavell
pages 13, 20, 47, 66, 100, 130, 141, 162, 167

Matt Russell
pages 21, 31, 35, 36, 39, 40, 48, 51, 52

Yuki Sugiura
pages 10-11, 55

Ian Wallace
page 4

Kate Whitaker
pages 6, 9, 22, 26, 57, 70, 73, 116, 123, 139, 148, 161, 170, 173

Isobel Wield
pages 102, 133

Clare Winfield
pages 14, 25, 38, 45, 69, 136, 165, 166, 174, 180